The Best Canadian Animal Stories

The Best Canadian Animal Stories

Classic Tales by Master Storytellers

Edited by

Muriel Whitaker

M&S

Canadian Cataloguing in Publication Data

Main entry under title:

The best Canadian animal stories : classic tales by master storytellers

ISBN 0-7710-8819-1

1. Animals – Fiction.   2. Short stories, Canadian (English).*   3. Canadian fiction (English) – 20th century.*   I. Whitaker, Muriel, 1923–   .

PS8323.A5B47   1997   C813'.0108'0362   C97-930309-5
PR9197.35.A5B47   1997

Illustrations by Brian Deines

Typesetting by M&S, Toronto
Printed and bound in Canada

McClelland & Stewart Inc.
The Canadian Publishers
481 University Avenue
Toronto, Ontario
M5G 2E9

1 2 3 4 5 6   02 01 00 99 98 97

For Karen and Ian

Contents

Introduction

In the essay which Charles G.D. Roberts prefaced to *The Kindred of the Wild* (1900), he pointed out that "the animal story, in one form or another, is as old as the beginnings of literature." From the hunting tales of early man and the fables in which animals represented particular virtues and vices to adventure stories and travellers' tales, animals played roles that were usually intended to highlight "the final triumph of the human actor." What distinguished Roberts' stories was their concern with "the psychology of animal life" and with a "search for the motive beneath the action." The realistic animal story, in Roberts' definition, is "a psychological romance constructed on a framework of natural science."

Charles G.D. Roberts and Ernest Thompson Seton developed almost simultaneously this genre which is Canada's original contribution to world literature. At the same time as the New Brunswick author was presenting in fictional form his efforts to "get under the skins" of his subjects, Seton was informing the readers of *Wild Animals I Have Known* (1898) that "the animals in this book were all real characters. They lived the lives I have depicted, and showed the stamp of heroism and personality more strongly by far than it has been in the power of my pen to tell." Roberts claimed priority over Seton for a "new departure in animal stories"; his first example, "Do Seek Their Meat from God," was published in *Harper's Monthly*, December 1892. However, it was Seton who first established a market for this kind of writing.

Given the plenitude of wild life that Europeans found here, it is not surprising that the country should have generated both literary and painterly responses. Henry Kelsey, probably the first white man to reach the prairies (1690-1692), recorded his impression in iambic pentameter: "This plain affords nothing but beast and grass." Alexander MacKenzie (1789) praised the abundance of "beaver, moose-deer, fallow-deer, elks, bears, buffalos etc." Dr. Walter Cheadle and William Fitzwilliam, Viscount Milton, on a trans-Canada journey in 1862-1863, rejoiced in the opportunities for sport: "hope to see bear," "shoot a turkey buzzard," "Get prairie hen and plover," "Mail stops for us to shoot a pheasant," "Milton and I start to run some fine white timber wolves," "Delighted with the news that buffalo bulls are within half a day."

The animals and birds are evidently regarded as inferior species in the Great Chain of Being. The explorers, traders, travellers and settlers appreciated the plentiful wildlife that ensured sport and a supply of food and clothing. Though they might fear the power of the beasts, encounters with bears, wolves, moose and buffalo allowed them to prove their manhood.

The original peoples whom the Europeans encountered, however, had an entirely different attitude to the natural world. Mythic agency rested not with a Christian God but with Coyote, Bear, Raven, Rabbit, Wolf and Mountain Goat. These powerful figures could speak, change their shapes, create and control the natural world. A few white men learned the rituals that provided access to supernatural power. An English explorer, Alexander Henry, who lived with prairie Indians between 1760 and 1776, described his hosts' reaction when he shot a bear:

> All my assistants approached and all, but particularly my old mother (as I was wont to call her) took her head in their hands, stroking and kissing it several times; begging a thousand pardons for taking away her life; calling her their relation and grandmother.

Archie Belaney (Grey Owl), who lived with the Ojibwa of the Bear Island band in 1908, learned to propitiate the beaver spirit as an aid to hunting. In her retelling of an Indian legend, "Master Rabbit and the Bad Wild Cat," Lady Crowe, writing under the name Peter Lum, captures this alternative view of the animal world.

The author of a realistic story uses techniques appropriate to fiction in order to differentiate the work from a naturalist's report of animal behaviour. The protagonist must be heroic, with superior attributes such as courage, determination, memory and reasoning power, to ensure success in the struggle for survival that characterized Charles Darwin's evolutionary theories. The bear's solicitude for her cubs, the coyote's loyalty to his friend, a dog, the crow's delight in his cherry tree swing, the responsibility which the stallion or the musk-ox feels for his herd's safety are traits that help define their personalities. They also provide motivations that facilitate plot development. The life histories which Roberts, Seton, Dickie, Batten and Dodds relate are punctuated with hazards that test the animal's quality and create suspense.

Among recurrent enemies is the villainous hunter armed with gun or trap; for example, Wood's Warty Sloane, Batten's Strychnine Loam, Seton's Old Cuddy with his bob-tailed yellow cur, and the beery young men of Burgeo in Mowat's story of the trapped whale. By an ironic reversal of the adventure story pattern, the successful hunter is perceived not as a hero but as a murderer. Harassing animals is a sign of moral deficiency. In the words of Wood's narrator, these "trashy people" suffer "forms of blindness that decent folk just won't tolerate." Successful writers so convincingly convey a sense of personality that the reader becomes intimately engaged in the fate of the animal hero.

An affinity between people and animals may be the basis for close emotional attachments. Loneliness, whether experienced in the underpopulated wilderness or impersonal city, fosters companionship. Grey Owl, in *Pilgrims of the Wild* (1935), describes the closeness that developed between himself and a beaver called Jelly Roll during a winter when "we were both, of our kind, alone." The beaver's attempts at communication and her co-operation in keeping up the home "strengthened indissolubly" their bonding. In *The Adventures of Sajo and Her Beaver People*, from which "Big Small and Little Small" is excerpted, the motherless native children, Sajo and Shapian, adopt the equally motherless beaver kittens, engaging in mutual exchanges of affection.

The British Columbia artist Emily Carr, beset by importunate lodgers, querulous sisters and unappreciative viewers, seems to have preferred animals to people. "Life's an awfully lonesome affair," she confided to her journal on July 16, 1933. Pets were a reliable source of entertainment, comfort and joy. On September 8 she was writing:

> Oh, what a joy this morning! Sun blazing, whole woods laughing, dogs hilarious. . . . The monk in her warm dress is sitting in the sun, replete with satisfaction. Susie the rat's pink nose keeps popping out from the front of my jacket.

And on September 12, 1934:

> Sometimes I think I'm not half grateful enough to the creatures. I wonder if my book with little sidelights on their lives will make animals any dearer or any clearer to anybody. I couldn't imagine a world without the love and the interest of them. They put up with you when nobody else will. In your very most hateful moods they still love you.

The Airedale that belongs to Hubert Evans' Ed was both a loyal companion and a link to the wild life surrounding their wilderness home. No Canadian writer has more philosophically described the bond between dog and owner than Bruce Hutchison in his last essay collection, *A Life in the Country* (1988):

> I had come, in my age, to believe that dogs as a rule are more shapely than men or women and more virtuous. Look into the eyes of a good dog and you will glimpse the infinite variety and possibilities of life. You will also be reminded that dog and man travel the same unmarked road to the great unknown, differing only in levels of intelligence by a pretty narrow margin. . . . Look again into the dog's eyes and you will observe their puzzlement, the longing search for reality behind the veil, the insoluble dilemma of all mankind.

Martha Brooks' sensitive story, "A Boy and His Dog," poignantly exemplifies Hutchison's perceptions.

In *The Voice from the Attic* (1960) Robertson Davies, reflecting on "some aspects of the world of books today," insists that good fiction "asks the reader to feel." He adds that the clerisy (his term for people who like to read books) "have reached that point of maturity where they know that thought and reason, unless matched by feeling, are empty, delusive things." Gladys F. Lewis' "The Black Stallion and the Red Mare," Kerry Wood's "The Dark-eyed Doe," Farley Mowat's "The Burgeo Whale," Gabrielle Roy's "Jeannot the Crow," Barbara Grantmyre's "Christmas Goose" and Alistair MacLeod's "Winter Dog" all show a sympathetic human involvement in animal life with which the reader can identify. Here is the benevolent face of Roberts' and Seton's harsh determinism. The human desire for an emotional response to literature may explain the popularity of animal stories among readers of all ages.

In the animal story genre, the story-teller's art conveys a sense not only of personality but also of habitat. "When Twilight Falls on the Stump Lots" opens with a description composed like a landscape painting. "A flood of sunset colour" illuminates the winter-whitened stumps, the greening hollows of early spring, the rich dark red of the newborn calf. It reveals the shapes of boulders and the ragged black wall of the fir wood, the texture of coarse grass and rough-mossed hillocks. The black-and-white cow's inability to harmonize with the landscape tones surrounding her precipitates the drama that follows. As well, the twilight of the title symbolizes the fate that brings the animals' lives so irrevocably and ingloriously to an end.

"Landscape just has an awful lot to do with literature," says Alistair MacLeod, and no Canadian writer has made more effective use of Nova Scotia's coastal landscape/seascape – the realm of "newness and the extraordinary." In "Winter Dog," centuries of maritime history are evoked as MacLeod describes the kegs of rum, the bloated horses, the fishing paraphernalia, the timber and furniture from wrecked ships that ended up in local houses, the bloated bodies of men swept overboard, the women and children saved by reaching life-lines, the dazed young sealers sheltered by local families. In particular, MacLeod's use of tactile imagery illuminates setting, character and event, enabling the reader to feel against the face the ice particles which the dog's paws dislodge as he pulls the boy on the sleigh, the coldness of the perspiration outlining the body in rime, the slide towards the black water, the snow blowing into eyes and almost freezing them shut, the shifting of ice under numbed feet, the deceptive warmth of the water when boy and dog fall through the "slob" ice, "thick and dense and soupy."

Reference to the seasonal cycle is a common technique for imposing an orderly structure on narrative. Spring is a season of birth and learning, a time when the dark-eyed doe produces her fawn "in a hidden part of the willow thickets." In summer the scarcely setting sun parches the Barrens' old caribou moss into "a brittle carpet dry as shaving"; a sinister flaming, a brilliant dawning at a wrong point of earth sends the musk-ox Umingmuk and all other life fleeing before it. Autumn presages death. Buddy takes his old dog for a last walk on the prairies; the brilliance of Indian summer makes the act a kind of apotheosis. Autumn also brings a new group of junior fellows to Massey College to fall in love and engage in fantastic creation. Snow shrouds the winter forest, driving Belette the Weasel on a fatal forage, while back in her rock den his mate, Gracilis, lies curled. Within her, six "minute specks" will become six young weasels by spring.

The lives of animals and birds are inextricably linked to habitat. Increasingly, as Donald G. Dodds' *Wild Captives* demonstrates, an animal's freedom can be turned into death because of the presence of humans. In *Remembering the Don* (1981), Charles Sauriol recalled that Ernest Thompson Seton, visiting the North Toronto ravines he had roamed as a boy and recreated in his fiction, found them in 1938 "almost as I knew them in 1874." By 1954 there was dereliction – the ravine's face marred by fill from Toronto subway digging, the creek no longer crystal clear, the construction of a freeway imminent and the wildlife dispersed.

In March 1994, *The Observer*, an authoritative London newspaper, announced that the planet's bird and animal species are disappearing at a rate of 11 per cent each decade. Two years later the International Union for the Conservation of Nature, meeting in Montreal, found that one hundred species per day are disappearing as habitats are destroyed. In Canada alone, calculates the World Wildlife Fund, at least 240 acres of wilderness disappear every hour because of logging, mining, hydro dams, city subdivisions and other commercial activities. About 8,000 species of plants and animals in our country are at risk; in 1996, 274 of them were on the endangered list – including the beluga whale, the short-eared owl, the Pacific water shrew, the cricket frog, the bearded seal, Ontario's northern bobwhite and British Columbia's Nuttall's cottontail.

The seventeen stories, many of them long out of print, which are collected in this anthology are intended to provide entertainment. They should also remind us of Bruce Hutchison's warning that "humans divorced from nature lose their vital juices."

When Twilight Falls
on the Stump Lots

◄○►

SIR CHARLES G.D. ROBERTS

Sir Charles G.D. Roberts (1860-1943), the son of an Anglican clergy-man, was born in Douglas, New Brunswick, and grew up in Westock, near the Tantramar Marshes. Though he spent most of his life in cities – Fredericton; Windsor, Nova Scotia (where he was Professor of English at King's College from 1885 to 1895); New York; London; and, after 1925, Toronto – he liked to call himself a backwoodsman. He was best known in his lifetime as a Romantic poet, and his efforts at realism are found only in his animal stories, many of them written between 1900 and 1907. For Roberts, the struggle of wild animals to survive dramatically encapsulated "the mystery of life and fate."

"When Twilight Falls on the Stump Lots," from Kindred of the Wild *(1900), exemplifies Roberts' contention that "within their*

varying limitations, animals can and do reason." The mother bear, motivated by hunger and maternal love, is credited with memories that help her to devise a strategic design. The cow is empowered by anger to respond. The vividly realized setting of the pioneer farm and scrupulously detailed description of the calf's behaviour derive from the author's boyhood experience. Defending himself against the charge that he was an "amateur" woodsman, Roberts wrote to Clarence Buel on October 26, 1908, that he had spent his "childhood and boyhood on a backwoods farm, shared in all the work of the woodsmen and never been to school till I was fourteen years old." The story's ironic conclusion illustrates the author's dislike of happy endings unrealistically manipulated. "In real life, more often," he told his friend Bliss Carman, "fate inexorably works the thing out to the bitter end." Other collections are The Watchers of the Trails *(1904),* More Kindred of the Wild *(1911),* Thirteen Bears *(1947) and* The Last Barrier and Other Stories *(1958).*

The wet, chill first of the spring, its blackness made tender by the lilac wash of the afterglow, lay upon the high, open stretches of the stump lots. The winter-whitened stumps, the sparse patches of juniper and bay just budding, the rough-mossed hillocks, the harsh boulders here and there up-thrusting from the soil, the swampy hollows wherein a coarse grass began to show green, all seemed anointed, as it were, to an ecstasy of peace by the chrism of that paradisial colour. Against the lucid immensity of the

April sky the thin tops of five or six soaring ram-pikes aspired like violet flames. Along the skirts of the stump lots a fir wood reared a ragged-crested wall of black against the red amber of the horizon.

Late that afternoon, beside a juniper thicket not far from the centre of the stump lots, a young black and white cow had given birth to her first calf. The little animal had been licked assiduously by the mother's caressing tongue till its colour began to show, of a rich dark red. Now it had struggled to its feet, and, with its dispro-portionately long, thick legs braced wide apart, was beginning to nurse. Its blunt wet muzzle and thick lips tugged eagerly, but some-what blunderingly as yet, at the unaccustomed teats; and its tail lifted, twitching with delight, as the first warm streams of mother milk went down its throat. It was a pathetically awkward, unlovely little figure, not yet advanced to that youngling winsomeness which is the heritage, to some degree and at some period, of the infancy of all the kindreds that breathe upon the earth. But to the young mother's eyes it was the most beautiful of things. With her head twisted far around, she nosed and licked its heaving flanks as it nursed; and between deep, ecstatic breathings she uttered in her throat low murmurs, unspeakably tender, of encouragement and caress. The delicate but pervading flood of sunset colour had the effect of blending the ruddy-hued calf into the tones of the land-scape; but the cow's insistent blotches of black and white stood out sharply, refusing to harmonize. The drench of violet light was of no avail to soften their staring contrasts. They made her vividly conspicuous across the whole breadth of the stump lots, to eyes that watched her from the forest coverts.

The eyes that watched her – long, fixedly, hungrily – were small and red. They belonged to a lank she-bear, whose gaunt flanks and rusty coat proclaimed a season of famine in the wilderness. She could not see the calf, which was hidden by a hillock and some juniper scrub, but its presence was very legibly conveyed to her by the mother's solicitous watchfulness. After a motionless scrutiny from behind the screen of fir branches, the lean bear stole noiselessly forth from the shadows into the great wash of violet light. Step by step, and very slowly, with the patience that endures because confident of its object, she crept toward that oasis of mothering joy in the vast emptiness of the stump lots. Now crouching, now crawling, turning to this side and to that, taking advantage of every hollow, of every thicket, every hillock, every aggressive stump, her craft succeeded in eluding even the wild and menacing watchfulness of the young mother's eyes.

The spring had been a trying one for the lank she-bear. Her den, in a dry tract of hemlock wood some furlongs back from the stump lots, was a snug little cave under the uprooted base of a lone pine, which had somehow grown up among the alien hemlocks only to draw down upon itself at last, by its superior height, the fury of a passing hurricane. The winter had contributed but scanty snowfall to cover the bear in her sleep; and the March thaws, unseasonably early and ardent, had called her forth to activity weeks too soon. Then frosts had come with belated severity, sealing away the budding tubers, which are the bear's chief dependence for spring diet; and worst of all, a long stretch of intervale meadow by the neighbouring river, which had once been rich in ground nuts, had been ploughed up the previous spring and subjected to the producing of oats and corn. When she was feeling the pinch of meagre rations, and when the fat which a liberal autumn of blueberries had laid up about her ribs was getting as shrunken as the last snow in the thickets, she gave birth to two hairless and hungry little cubs. They were very blind, and ridiculously small to be born of so big a mother; and having so much growth to make during the next few months, their appetites were immeasurable. They tumbled, and squealed, and tugged at their mother's teats, and grew astonishingly, and made huge haste to cover their bodies with fur of a soft and silken black; and all this vitality of theirs made a strenuous demand upon their mother's milk. There were no more bee-trees left in the neighbourhood. The long wanderings which she was forced to take in her search for roots and tubers were in themselves a drain upon her nursing powers. At last, reluctant though she was to attract the hostile notice of the settlement, she found herself forced to hunt on the borders of the sheep pastures. Before all else in life was it important to her that these two tumbling little ones in the den should not go hungry. Their eyes were open now – small and dark and whimsical, their ears quaintly large and inquiring for their roguish little faces. Had she not been driven by the unkind season to so much hunting and foraging, she would have passed near all her time rapturously in the den under the pine root, fondling those two soft miracles of her world.

With the killing of three lambs – at widely scattered points, so as to mislead retaliation – things grew a little easier for the harassed bear; and presently she grew bolder in tampering with the creatures under man's protection. With one swift, secret blow of her mighty paw she struck down a young ewe which had strayed within reach of her hiding-place. Dragging her prey deep into the woods, she fared well upon it for some days, and was happy with her growing cubs. It was just when she had begun to feel the fasting which came upon the exhaustion of this store that, in a hungry hour, she sighted the conspicuous markings of the black and white cow.

It is altogether unusual for the black bear of the eastern woods to attack any quarry so large as a cow, unless under the spur of fierce hunger or fierce rage. The she-bear was powerful beyond her fellows. She had the strongest possible incentive to bold hunting, and she had lately grown confident beyond her wont. Nevertheless, when she began her careful stalking of this big game which she coveted, she had no definite intention of forcing a battle with the cow. She had observed that cows, accustomed to the protection of man, would at times leave their calves asleep and stray off some distance in their pasturing. She had even seen calves left all by themselves in a field, from morning till night, and had wondered at such negligence in their mothers. Now she had a confident idea that sooner or later the calf would lie down to sleep, and the young mother roam a little wide in search of the scant young grass. Very softly, very self-effacingly, she crept nearer step by step, following up the wind, till at last, undiscovered, she was crouching behind a thick patch of juniper, on the slope of a little hollow not ten paces distant from the cow and the calf.

By this time the tender violet light was fading to a greyness over hillock and hollow; and with the deepening of the twilight the faint breeze, which had been breathing from the northward, shifted suddenly and came in slow, warm pulsations out of the south. At the same time the calf, having nursed sufficiently, and feeling his baby legs tired of the weight they had not yet learned to carry, laid himself down. On this the cow shifted her position. She turned half round, and lifted her head high. As she did so a scent of

peril was borne in upon her fine nostrils. She recognized it instantly. With a snort of anger she sniffed again; then stamped a challenge with her fore hoofs, and levelled the lance-points of her horns toward the menace. The next moment her eyes, made keen by the fear of love, detected the black outline of the bear's head through the coarse screen of the juniper. Without a second's hesitation, she flung up her tail, gave a short bellow, and charged.

The moment she saw herself detected, the bear rose upon her hindquarters; nevertheless she was in a measure surprised by the sudden blind fury of the attack. Nimbly she swerved to avoid it, aiming at the same time a stroke with her mighty forearm, which, if it had found its mark, would have smashed her adversary's neck. But as she struck out, in the act of shifting her position, a depression of the ground threw her off her balance. The next instant one sharp horn caught her slantingly in the flank, ripping its way upward and inward, while the mad impact threw her upon her back.

Grappling, she had her assailant's head and shoulders in a trap, and her gigantic claws cut through the flesh and sinew like knives; but at the desperate disadvantage of her position she could inflict no disabling blow. The cow, on the other hand, though mutilated and streaming with blood, kept pounding with her whole massive weight, and with short tremendous shocks crushing the breath from her foe's ribs.

Presently, wrenching herself free, the cow drew off for another battering charge; and as she did so the bear hurled herself violently down the slope, and gained her feet behind a dense thicket of bay shrub. The cow, with one eye blinded and the other obscured by blood, glared around for her in vain, then, in a panic of mother terror, plunged back to her calf.

Snatching at the respite, the bear crouched down, craving that invisibility which is the most faithful shield of the furtive kindred. Painfully, and leaving a drenched red trail behind her, she crept off from the disastrous neighbourhood. Soon the deepening twilight sheltered her. But she could not make haste; and she knew that death was close upon her.

Once within the woods, she struggled straight toward the den that held her young. She hungered to die licking them. But destiny is as implacable as iron to the wilderness people, and even this was denied her. Just a half score of paces from the lair in the pine root, her hour descended upon her. There was a sudden redder and fuller gush upon the trail, the last light of longing faded out of her eyes; and she lay down upon her side.

The merry little cubs within the den were beginning to expect her, and getting restless. As the night wore on, and no mother came, they ceased to be merry. By morning they were shivering with hunger and desolate fear. But the doom of the ancient wood was less harsh than its wont, and spared them some days of starving anguish; for about noon a pair of foxes discovered the dead mother, astutely estimated the situation, and then, with the boldness of good appetite, made their way into the unguarded den.

As for the red calf, its fortune was ordinary. Its mother, for all her wounds, was able to nurse and cherish it through the night; and with morning came a searcher from the farm and took it, with the bleeding mother, safely back to the settlement. There it was tended and fattened, and within a few weeks found its way to the cool marble slabs of a city market.

Redruff: The Story of
the Don Valley Partridge

◄o►

ERNEST THOMPSON SETON

Ernest Thompson Seton (1860-1946) was born near Durham, England. When he was five years old, the family emigrated to Canada, where they lived on a farm at Lindsay, Ontario, and then in Toronto. Like many wildlife writers, he had an eclectic career. Trained as a painter, he was a Manitoba homesteader, naturalist, author and lecturer. After 1896 he lived in the United States, writing, lecturing and founding an outdoor organization for boys, the Woodcraft Indians, which anticipated the Boy Scout movement.

His first book, Wild Animals I Have Known *(1898), included a "Note to the Reader" which explained the author's approach:*

These stories are true. Although I have left the strict lines of historical truth in many places, the animals in this book were all real characters. They lived the lives I have depicted, and showed the stamp of heroism and personality more strongly by far than it has been in my power to tell . . . . The real personality of the individual, and his view of life are my theme.

In "Redruff, the Story of the Don Valley Partridge," Seton recreates the area of the Don Valley and the Rosedale Ravine, of Sugar Loaf, Castle Frank and Mud Creek, to which as a boy he had escaped from an unhappy home. It was a place where he could observe the habits and habitats of abundant wildlife, as well as the "labor and ingenuity" that men put into destroying wild animals. Redruff was an actual bird that "really lived in the Don Valley north of Toronto, and many of my companions will remember him. He was killed in 1889, between the Sugar Loaf and Castle Frank, by a creature whose name I have withheld as it is the species, rather than the individual that I wish to expose."

This partridge is a typical animal hero, superior in the size, intelligence, obedience and beauty essential for survival. Seton skilfully depicts the setting in terms of its usefulness in providing food and shelter; we see the crystal brook, a curl of birch-bark, a sandy bank screened by brambles, a great pine log on the sunlit edge of the beaver meadow and a frozen snowdrift from the bird's perspective. Yet in spite of instinct or reason or natural advantages, three generations progress inexorably towards death, as, the weakest first, they succumb to a variety of threats. Seton explains, "The fact that these stories are true is the reason why all are tragic.

The life of a wild animal always has a tragic end." *Seton's other works include* The Biography of a Grizzly *(1907),* The Biography of a Silver Fox *(1909),* The Two Little Savages *(1911) and* Famous Animal Stories *(1934).*

◄O►

I

Down the wooded slope of Taylor's Hill the Mother Partridge led her brood; down toward the crystal brook that by some strange whim was called Mud Creek. Her little ones were one day old but already quick on foot, and she was taking them for the first time to drink.

She walked slowly, crouching low as she went, for the woods were full of enemies. She was uttering a soft little cluck in her throat, a call to the little balls of mottled down that on their tiny pink legs came toddling after, and peeping softly and plaintively if left even a few inches behind, and seeming so fragile they made the very chickadees look big and coarse. There were twelve of them, but Mother Grouse watched them all, and she watched every bush and tree and thicket, and the whole woods and the sky itself. Always for enemies she seemed seeking – friends were too scarce to be looked for – and an enemy she found. Away across the level beaver meadow was a great brute of a fox. He was coming their way, and in a few moments would surely wind them or strike their trail. There was no time to lose.

'*Krrr! Krrr!*' (Hide! Hide!) cried the mother in a low firm voice, and the little bits of things, scarcely bigger than acorns and but a day old, scattered far (a few inches) apart to hide. One dived under a leaf, another between two roots, a third crawled into a curl of birch-bark, a fourth into a hole, and so on, till all were hidden but one who could find no cover, so squatted on a broad yellow chip and lay very flat, and closed his eyes very tight, sure that now he was safe from being seen. They ceased their frightened peeping and all was still.

Mother Partridge flew straight toward the dreaded beast, alighted fearlessly a few yards to one side of him, and then flung herself on the ground, flopping as though winged and lame – oh, so dreadfully lame – and whining like a distressed puppy. Was she begging for mercy – mercy from a bloodthirsty, cruel fox? Oh, dear no! She was no fool. One often hears of the cunning of the fox. Wait and see what a fool he is compared with a mother-partridge. Elated at the prize so suddenly within his reach, the fox turned with a dash and caught – at least, no, he didn't quite catch the bird; she flopped by chance just a foot out of reach. He followed with another jump and would have seized her this time surely, but somehow a sapling came just between, and the partridge dragged herself awkwardly away and under a log, but the great brute snapped his jaws and bounded over the log, while she, seeming a trifle less lame, made another clumsy forward spring and tumbled down a bank, and Reynard, keenly following, almost caught her tail, but, oddly enough, fast as he went and leaped, she still seemed just a trifle faster. It was most extraordinary. A winged partridge and he, Reynard, the Swift-foot, had not caught her in five minutes' racing. It was really shameful. But the partridge seemed to gain strength as the fox put forth his, and after a quarter of a mile race, racing that was somehow all away from Taylor's Hill, the bird got unaccountably quite well, and, rising with a derisive whirr, flew off through the woods leaving the fox utterly dumfounded to realize that he had been made a fool of, and, worst of all, he now remembered that this was not the first time he had been served this very trick, though he never knew the reason for it.

Meanwhile Mother Partridge skimmed in a great circle and came by a roundabout way back to the little fuzz-balls she had left hidden in the woods.

With a wild bird's keen memory for places, she went to the very grass-blade she last trod on, and stood for a moment fondly to admire the perfect stillness of her children. Even at her step not one had stirred, and the little fellow on the chip, not so very badly concealed after all, had not budged, nor did he now; he only closed his eyes a tiny little bit harder, till the mother said:

'*K-reet!*' (Come, children) and instantly like a fairy story, every hole gave up its little baby-partridge, and the wee fellow on the chip, the biggest of them all really, opened his big-little eyes and ran to the shelter of her broad tail, with a sweet little '*peep peep*' which an enemy could not have heard three feet away, but which his mother could not have missed thrice as far, and all the other thimblefuls of down joined in, and no doubt thought themselves dreadfully noisy, and were proportionately happy.

The sun was hot now. There was an open space to cross on the road to the water, and, after a careful lookout for enemies, the mother gathered the little things under the shadow of her spread fantail and kept off all danger of sunstroke until they reached the brier thicket by the stream.

Here a cottontail rabbit leaped out and gave them a great scare. But the flag of truce he carried behind was enough. He was an old friend; and among other things the little ones learned that day that Bunny always sails under a flag of truce, and lives up to it too.

And then came the drink, the purest of living water, though silly men had called it Mud Creek.

At first the little fellows didn't know how to drink, but they copied their mother, and soon learned to drink like her and give thanks after every sip. There they stood in a row along the edge, twelve little brown and golden balls on twenty-four little pink-toed, in-turned feet, with twelve sweet little golden heads gravely bowing, drinking and giving thanks like their mother.

Then she led them by short stages, keeping the cover, to the far side of the beaver-meadow, where was a great grassy dome. The mother had made a note of this dome some time before. It takes a number of such domes to raise a brood of partridges. For this was an ant's nest. The old one stepped on top, looked about a moment, then gave half a dozen vigorous rakes with her claws. The friable ant-hill was broken open, and the earthen galleries scattered in ruins down the slope. The ants swarmed out and quarrelled with each other for lack of a better plan. Some ran around the hill with vast energy and little purpose, while a few of the more sensible began to carry away fat white eggs. But the old partridge, coming to the little ones, picked up one of these juicy-looking bags and clucked and dropped it, and picked it up again and again and clucked, then swallowed it. The young ones stood around, then one little yellow fellow, the one that sat on the chip, picked up an ant-egg, dropped it a few times, then yielding to a sudden impulse, swallowed it, and so had learned to eat. Within twenty minutes even the runt had learned, and a merry time they had scrambling after the delicious eggs as their mother broke open more ant-galleries, and sent them and their contents rolling down the bank, till every little partridge had so crammed his little crop that he was positively misshapen and could eat no more.

Then all went cautiously up the stream, and on a sandy bank, well screened by brambles, they lay for all that afternoon, and learned how pleasant it was to feel the cool powdery dust running between their hot little toes. With their strong bent for copying, they lay on their sides like their mother and scratched with their tiny feet and flopped with their wings, though they had no wings to flop with, only a little tag among the down on each side, to show where the wings would come. That night she took them to a dry thicket near by, and there among the crisp, dead leaves that would prevent an enemy's silent approach on foot, and under the inter-lacing briers that kept off all foes of the air, she cradled them in their feather-shingled nursery and rejoiced in the fulness of a mother's joy over the wee cuddling things that peeped in their sleep and snuggled so trustfully against her warm body.

II

The third day the chicks were much stronger on their feet. They no longer had to go around an acorn; they could even scramble over pine-cones, and on the little tags that marked the places for their wings, were now to be seen blue rows of fat blood-quills.

Their start in life was a good mother, good legs, a few reliable instincts, and a germ of reason. It was instinct, that is, inherited habit, which taught them to hide at the word from their mother; it was instinct that taught them to follow her, but it was reason which made them keep under the shadow of her tail when the sun was smiling down, and from that day reason entered more and more into their expanding lives.

Next day the blood-quills had sprouted the tips of feathers. On the next, the feathers were well out, and a week later the whole family of down-clad babies were strong on the wing.

And yet not all – poor little Runtie had been sickly from the first. He bore his half-shell on his back for hours after he came out; he ran less and cheeped more than his brothers, and when one evening at the onset of a skunk the mother gave the word '*Kwit, kwit*' (Fly, fly), Runtie was left behind, and when she gathered her brood on the piney hill he was missing, and they saw him no more.

Meanwhile, their training had gone on. They knew that the finest grasshoppers abounded in the long grass by the brook; they knew that the currant-bushes dropped fatness in the form of smooth, green worms; they knew that the dome of an ant-hill rising against the distant woods stood for a garner of plenty; they knew that strawberries, though not really insects, were almost as delicious; they knew that the huge danaid butterflies were good, safe game, if they could only catch them, and that a slab of bark dropping from the side of a rotten log was sure to abound in good things of many different kinds; and they had learned, also, that yellow-jackets, mud-wasps, woolly worms, and hundred-leggers were better let alone.

It was now July, the Moon of Berries. The chicks had grown and flourished amazingly during this last month, and were now so large that in her efforts to cover them the mother was kept standing all night.

They took their daily dust-bath, but of late had changed to another higher on the hill. It was one in use by many different birds, and at first the mother disliked the idea of such a second-hand bath. But the dust was of such a fine, agreeable quality, and the children led the way with such enthusiasm, that she forgot her mistrust.

After a fortnight the little ones began to droop and she herself did not feel very well. They were always hungry, and though they ate enormously, they one and all grew thinner and thinner. The mother was the last to be affected. But when it came, it came as hard on her – a ravenous hunger, a feverish headache, and a wasting weakness. She never knew the cause. She could not know that the dust of the much-used dust-bath, that her true instinct taught her to mistrust at first, and now again to shun, was sown with parasitic worms, and that all of the family were infested.

No natural impulse is without a purpose. The mother-bird's knowledge of healing was only to follow natural impulse. The eager, feverish craving for something, she knew not what, led her to eat, or try, everything that looked eatable and to seek the coolest woods. And there she found a deadly sumach laden with its poison fruit. A month ago she would have passed it by, but now she tried the unattractive berries. The acrid burning juice seemed to answer some strange demand of her body; she ate and ate, and all her family joined in the strange feast of physic. No human doctor could have hit it better; it proved a biting, drastic purge, the dreadful secret foe was downed, the danger passed. But not for all – Nature, the old nurse, had come too late for two of them. The weakest, by inexorable law, dropped out. Enfeebled by the disease, the remedy was too severe for them. They drank and drank by the stream, and next morning did not move when the others followed the mother. Strange vengeance was theirs now, for a skunk, the same that could have told where Runtie went, found and devoured their bodies and died of the poison they had eaten.

Seven little partridges now obeyed the mother's call. Their individual characters were early shown and now developed fast. The weaklings were gone, but there were still a fool and a lazy one. The mother could not help caring for some more than for others, and her favorite was the biggest, he who once sat on the yellow chip for concealment. He was not only the biggest, strongest, and handsomest of the brood, but best of all, the most obedient. His mother's warning 'rrrrr' (danger) did not always keep the others from a risky path or a doubtful food, but obedience seemed natural to him, and he never failed to respond to her soft 'K-reet' (Come), and of this obedience he reaped the reward, for his days were longest in the land.

August, the Molting Moon, went by; the young ones were now three parts grown. They knew just enough to think themselves wonderfully wise. When they were small it was necessary to sleep on the ground so their mother could shelter them, but now they were too big to need that, and the mother began to introduce grown-up ways of life. It was time to roost in the trees. The young weasels, foxes, skunks, and minks were beginning to run. The ground grew more dangerous each night, so at sundown Mother Partridge called 'K-reet,' and flew into a thick, low tree.

The little ones followed, except one, an obstinate little fool who persisted in sleeping on the ground as heretofore. It was all right that time, but the next night his brothers were awakened by his cries. There was a slight scuffle, then stillness, broken only by a horrid sound of crunching bones and a smacking of lips. They peered down into the terrible darkness below, where the glint of two close-set eyes and a peculiar musty smell told them that a mink was the killer of their fool brother.

Six little partridges now sat in a row at night, with their mother in the middle, though it was not unusual for some little one with cold feet to perch on her back.

Their education went on, and about this time they were taught 'whirring.' A partridge can rise on the wing silently if it wishes, but whirring is so important at times that all are taught how and when to rise on thundering wings. Many ends are gained by the whirr. It warns all other partridges near that danger is at hand, it unnerves the gunner, or it fixes the foe's attention on the whirrer, while the others sneak off in silence, or by squatting, escape notice.

A partridge adage might well be 'foes and food for every moon.' September came, with seeds and grain in place of berries and ant-eggs, and gunners in place of skunks and minks.

The partridges knew well what a fox was, but had scarcely seen a dog. A fox they knew they could easily baffle by taking to a tree, but when in the Gunner Moon old Cuddy came prowling through the ravine with his bob-tailed yellow cur, the mother spied the dog and cried out, '*Kwit! kwit!*' (Fly, fly). Two of the brood thought it a pity their mother should lose her wits so easily over a fox, and were pleased to show their superior nerve by springing into a tree in spite of her earnestly repeated '*Kwit! kwit!*' and her example of speeding away on silent wings.

Meanwhile, the strange bob-tailed fox came under the tree and yapped and yapped at them. They were much amused at him and at their mother and brothers, so much so that they never noticed a rustling in the bushes till there was a loud *Bang! bang!* and down fell two bloody, flopping partridges, to be seized and mangled by the yellow cur until the gunner ran from the bushes and rescued the remains.

III

Cuddy lived in a wretched shanty near the Don, north of Toronto. His was what Greek philosophy would have demonstrated to be an ideal existence. He had no wealth, no taxes, no social pretensions, and no property to speak of. His life was made up of a very little work and a great deal of play, with as much out-door life as he chose. He considered himself a true sportsman because he was 'fond o' huntin',' and 'took a sight o' comfort out of seein' the critters hit the mud' when his gun was fired. The neighbors called him a squatter, and looked on him merely as an anchored tramp. He shot and trapped the year round, and varied his game somewhat with the season perforce, but had been heard to remark he could tell the month by the 'taste o' the patridges,' if he didn't happen to know by the almanac. This, no doubt, showed keen observation, but was also unfortunate proof of something not so creditable. The lawful season for murdering partridges began September 15th, but there was nothing surprising in Cuddy's being out a fortnight ahead of time. Yet he managed to escape punishment year after year, and even contrived to pose in a newspaper interview as an interesting character.

He rarely shot on the wing, preferring to pot his birds, which was not easy to do when the leaves were on, and accounted for the brood in the third ravine going so long unharmed; but the near prospect of other gunners finding them now, had stirred him to go after 'a mess o' birds.' He had heard no roar of wings when the mother-bird led off her four survivors, so pocketed the two he had killed and returned to the shanty.

The little grouse thus learned that a dog is not a fox, and must be differently played; and an old lesson was yet more deeply graven – 'Obedience is long life.'

The rest of September was passed in keeping quietly out of the way of gunners as well as some old enemies. They still roosted on the long thin branches of the hardwood trees among the thickest leaves, which protected them from foes in the air; the height saved them from foes on the ground, and left them nothing to fear but coons, whose slow, heavy tread on the limber boughs never failed to give them timely warning. But the leaves were falling now – every month its foes and its food. This was nut time, and it was owl time, too. Barred owls coming down from the north doubled or trebled the owl population. The nights were getting frosty and the coons less dangerous, so the mother changed the place of roosting to the thickest foliage of a hemlock-tree.

Only one of the brood disregarded the warning '*Kreet, kreet.*' He stuck to his swinging elm-bough, now nearly naked, and a great yellow-eyed owl bore him off before morning.

Mother and three young ones now were left, but they were as big as she was; indeed one, the eldest, he of the chip, was bigger. Their ruffs had begun to show. Just the tips, to tell what they would be like when grown, and not a little proud they were of them.

The ruff is to the partridge what the train is to the peacock – his chief beauty and his pride. A hen's ruff is black with a slight green gloss. A cock's is much larger and blacker and is glossed with more vivid bottle-green. Once in a while a partridge is born of unusual size and vigor, whose ruff is not only larger, but by a peculiar kind of intensification is of a deep coppery red, iridescent with violet, green, and gold. Such a bird is sure to be a wonder to all who know him, and the little one who had squatted on the chip, and had always done what he was told, developed before the Acorn Moon had changed, into all the glory of a gold and copper ruff – for this was Redruff, the famous partridge of the Don Valley.

IV

One day late in the Acorn Moon, that is, about mid-October, as the grouse family were basking with full crops near a great pine log on the sunlit edge of the beaver-meadow, they heard the far-away bang of a gun, and Redruff, acting on some impulse from within, leaped on the log, strutted up and down a couple of times, then, yielding to the elation of the bright, clear, bracing air, he whirred his wings in loud defiance. Then, giving fuller vent to this expression of vigor, just as a colt frisks to show how well he feels, he whirred yet more loudly, until, unwittingly, he found himself drumming, and tickled with the discovery of his new power, thumped the air again and again till he filled the near woods with the loud tattoo of the fully grown cock-partridge. His brother and sister heard and looked on with admiration and surprise; so did his mother, but from that time she began to be a little afraid of him.

In early November comes the moon of a weird foe. By a strange law of nature, not wholly without parallel among mankind, all partridges go crazy in the November moon of their first year. They become possessed of a mad hankering to get away somewhere, it does not matter much where. And the wisest of them do all sorts of foolish things at this period. They go drifting, perhaps, at speed over the country by night, and are cut in two by wires, or dash into lighthouses, or locomotive headlights. Daylight finds them in all sorts of absurd places, in buildings, in open marshes, perched on telephone wires in a great city, or even on board of coasting vessels. The craze seems to be a relic of a bygone habit of migration, and it has at least one good effect, it breaks up the families and prevents the constant intermarrying, which would surely be fatal to their race. It always takes the young badly their first year, and they may have it again the second fall, for it is very catching; but in the third season it is practically unknown.

Redruff's mother knew it was coming as soon as she saw the frost grapes blackening, and the maples shedding their crimson and gold. There was nothing to do but care for their health and keep them in the quietest part of the woods.

The first sign of it came when a flock of wild geese went *honking* southward overhead. The young ones had never before seen such long-necked hawks, and were afraid of them. But seeing that their mother had no fear, they took courage, and watched them with intense interest. Was it the wild, clanging cry that moved them, or was it solely the inner prompting then come to the surface? A strange longing to follow took possession of each of the young ones. They watched those arrowy trumpeters fading away to the south, and sought out higher perches to watch them farther yet, and from that time things were no more the same. The November moon was waxing, and when it was full, the November madness came.

The least vigorous of the flock were most affected. The little family was scattered. Redruff himself flew on several long erratic night journeys. The impulse took him southward, but there lay the boundless stretch of Lake Ontario, so he turned again, and the waning of the Mad Moon found him once more in the Mud Creek Glen, but absolutely alone.

V

Food grew scarce as winter wore on. Redruff clung to the old ravine and the piney sides of Taylor's Hill, but every month brought its food and its foes. The Mad Moon brought madness, solitude, and grapes; the Snow Moon came with rosehips; and the Stormy Moon brought browse of birch and silver storms that sheathed the woods in ice, and made it hard to keep one's perch while pulling off the frozen buds. Redruff's beak grew terribly worn with the work, so that even when closed there was still an opening through behind the hook. But nature had prepared him for the slippery footing; his toes, so slim and trim in September, had sprouted rows of sharp, horny points, and these grew with the growing cold, till the first snow had found him fully equipped with snow-shoes and ice-creepers. The cold weather had driven away most of the hawks and owls, and made it impossible for his four-footed enemies to approach unseen, so that things were nearly balanced.

His flight in search of food had daily led him farther on, till he had discovered and explored the Rosedale Creek, with its banks of silver-birch, and Castle Frank, with its grapes and rowan berries, as well as Chester woods, where amel-anchier and Virginia-creeper swung their fruit-bunches, and checkerberries glowed beneath the snow.

He soon found out that for some strange reason men with guns did not go within the high fence of Castle Frank. So among these scenes he lived his life, learning new places, new foods, and grew wiser and more beautiful every day.

He was quite alone so far as kindred were concerned, but that scarcely seemed a hardship. Wherever he went he could see the jolly chickadees scrambling merrily about, and he remembered the time when they had seemed such big, important creatures. They were the most absurdly cheerful things in the woods. Before the autumn was fairly over they had begun to sing their famous refrain, '*Spring Soon*,' and kept it up with good heart more or less all through the winter's direst storms, till at length the waning of the Hunger Moon, our February, seemed really to lend some point to the ditty, and they redoubled their optimistic announcement to the world in an 'I-told-you-so' mood. Soon good support was found, for the sun gained strength and melted the snow from the southern slope of Castle Frank Hill, and exposed great banks of fragrant wintergreen, whose berries were a bounteous feast for Redruff, and, ending the hard work of pulling frozen browse, gave his bill the needed chance to grow into its proper shape again. Very soon the first bluebird came flying over and warbled as he flew '*The spring is coming*.' The sun kept gaining, and early one day in the dark of the Wakening Moon of March there was a loud '*Caw, caw*,' and old Silverspot, the king-crow, came swinging along from the south at the head of his troops and officially announced

'THE SPRING HAS COME.'

All nature seemed to respond to this, the opening of the birds' New Year, and yet it was something within that chiefly seemed to move them. The chickadees went simply wild; they sang their '*Spring now, spring now now – Spring now now*,' so persistently that one wondered how they found time to get a living.

And Redruff felt it thrill him through and through. He sprang with joyous vigor on a stump and sent rolling down the little valley, again and again, a thundering '*Thump, thump, thump, thunderrrrrrrr*,' that wakened dull echoes as it rolled, and voiced his gladness in the coming of the spring.

Away down the valley was Cuddy's shanty. He heard the drum-call on the still morning air and 'reckoned there was a cock patridge to git,' and came sneaking up the ravine with his gun. But Redruff skimmed away in silence, nor rested till once more in Mud Creek Glen. And there he mounted the very log where first he had drummed and rolled his loud tattoo again and again, till a small boy who had taken a short cut to the mill through the woods, ran home, badly scared, to tell his mother he was sure the Indians were on the war-path, for he heard their war-drums beating in the glen.

Why does a happy boy holla? Why does a lonesome youth sigh? They don't know any more than Redruff knew why every day now he mounted some dead log and thumped and thundered to the woods; then strutted and admired his gorgeous blazing ruffs as they flashed their jewels in the sunlight, and then thundered out again. Whence now came the strange wish for someone else to admire the plumes? And why had such a notion never come till the Pussywillow Moon?

'*Thump, thump, thunder-r-r-r-r-rrrr*'
'*Thump, thump, thunder-r-r-r-r-rrrr*'
he rumbled again and again.

Day after day he sought the favorite log, and a new beauty, a rose-red comb, grew out above each clear, keen eye, and the clumsy snow-shoes were wholly shed from his feet. His ruff grew finer, his eye brighter, and his whole appearance splendid to behold, as he strutted and flashed in the sun. But – oh! he was *so lonesome now.*

Yet what could he do but blindly vent his hankering in this daily drum-parade, till on a day early in loveliest May, when the trilliums had fringed his log with silver stars, and he had drummed and longed, then drummed again, his keen ear caught a sound, a gentle footfall in the brush. He turned to a statue and watched; he knew he had been watched. Could it be possible? Yes! there it was – a form – another – a shy little lady grouse, now bashfully seeking to hide. In a moment he was by her side. His whole nature swamped by a new feeling – burnt up with thirst – a cooling spring in sight. And how he spread and flashed his proud array! How came he to know that that would please? He puffed his plumes and contrived to stand just right to catch the sun, and strutted and uttered a low, soft chuckle that must have been just as good as the 'sweet nothings' of another race, for clearly now her heart was won. Won, really, days ago, if only he had known. For full three days she had come at the loud tattoo and coyly admired him from afar, and felt a little piqued that he had not yet found out her, so close at hand. So it was not quite all mischance, perhaps, that little stamp that caught his ear. But now she meekly

bowed her head with sweet, submissive grace – the desert passed, the parch-burnt wanderer found the spring at last.

Oh, those were bright, glad days in the lovely glen of the unlovely name. The sun was never so bright, and the piney air was balmier sweet than dreams. And that great noble bird came daily on his log, sometimes with her and sometimes quite alone, and drummed for very joy of being alive. But why sometimes alone? Why not forever with his Brownie bride? Why should she stay to feast and play with him for hours, then take some stealthy chance to slip away and see him no more for hours or till next day, when his martial music from the log announced him restless for her quick return? There was a woodland mystery here he could not clear. Why should her stay with him grow daily less till it was down to minutes, and one day at last she never came at all. Nor the next, nor the next, and Redruff, wild, careered on lightning wing and drummed on the old log, then away up-stream on another log, and skimmed the hill to another ravine to drum and drum. But on the fourth day, when he came and loudly called her, as of old, at their earliest tryst, he heard a sound in the bushes, as at first, and there was his missing Brownie bride with ten little peeping partridges following after.

Redruff skimmed to her side, terribly frightening the bright-eyed downlings, and was just a little dashed to find the brood with claims far stronger than his own. But he soon accepted the change, and thenceforth joined himself to the brood, caring for them as his father never had for him.

VI

Good fathers are rare in the grouse world. The mother-grouse builds her nest and hatches out her young without help. She even hides the place of the nest from the father and meets him only at the drum-log and the feeding-ground, or perhaps the dusting-place, which is the club-house of the grouse kind.

When Brownie's little ones came out they had filled her every thought, even to the forgetting of their splendid father. But on the third day, when they were strong enough, she had taken them with her at the father's call.

Some fathers take no interest in their little ones, but Redruff joined at once to help Brownie in the task of rearing the brood. They had learned to eat and drink just as their father had learned long ago, and could toddle along, with their mother leading the way, while the father ranged near by or followed far behind.

The very next day, as they went from the hill-side down toward the creek in a somewhat drawn-out string, like beads with a big one at each end, a red squirrel, peeping around a pine-trunk, watched the procession of downlings with the Runtie straggling far in the rear. Redruff, yards behind, preening his feathers on a high log, had escaped the eye of the squirrel, whose strange perverted thirst for birdling blood was roused at what seemed so fair a chance. With murderous intent to cut off the hindmost straggler, he made a dash. Brownie could not have seen him until too late, but Redruff did. He flew for that red-haired cutthroat; his weapons were his fists, that is, the knob-joints of the wings, and what a blow he could strike! At the first onset he struck the squirrel square on the end of the nose, his weakest spot, and sent him reeling; he staggered and wriggled into a brush-pile, where he had expected to carry the little grouse, and there lay gasping with red drops trickling down his wicked snout. The partridges left him lying there, and what became of him they never knew, but he troubled them no more.

The family went on toward the water, but a cow had left deep tracks in the sandy loam, and into one of these fell one of the chicks and peeped in dire distress when he found he could not get out.

This was a fix. Neither old one seemed to know what to do, but as they trampled vainly round the edge, the sandy bank caved in, and, running down, formed a long slope, up which the young one ran and rejoined his brothers under the broad veranda of their mother's tail.

Brownie was a bright little mother, of small stature, but keen of wit and sense, and was, night and day, alert to care for her darling chicks. How proudly she stepped and clucked through the arching woods with her dainty brood behind her; how she strained her little brown tail almost to a half-circle to give them a broader shade, and never flinched at sight of any foe, but held ready to fight or fly, whichever seemed the best for her little ones.

Before the chicks could fly they had a meeting with old Cuddy; though it was June, he was out with his gun. Up the third ravine he went, and Tike, his dog, ranging ahead, came so dangerously near the Brownie brood that Redruff ran to meet him, and by the old but never failing trick led him on a foolish chase away back down the valley of the Don.

But Cuddy, as it chanced, came right along, straight for the brood, and Brownie, giving the signal to the children, '*Krrr, krrr*' (Hide, hide), ran to lead the man away just as her mate had led the dog. Full of a mother's devoted love, and skilled in the learning of the woods, she ran in silence till quite near, then sprang with a roar of wings right in his face, and tumbling on the leaves she shammed a lameness that for a moment deceived the poacher. But when she dragged one wing and whined about his feet, then slowly crawled away, he knew just what it meant – that it was all a trick to lead him from her brood, and he struck at her a savage blow; but little Brownie was quick, she avoided the blow and limped behind a sapling, there to beat herself upon the leaves again in sore distress, and seem so lame that Cuddy made another try to strike her down with a stick. But she moved in time to balk him, and bravely, steadfast still to lead him from her helpless little ones, she flung herself before him and beat her gentle breast upon the ground, and moaned as though begging for mercy. And Cuddy, failing again to strike her, raised his gun, and firing charge enough to kill a bear, he blew poor brave, devoted Brownie into quivering, bloody rags.

This gunner brute knew the young must be biding near, so looked about to find them. But no one moved or peeped. He saw not one, but as he tramped about with heedless, hateful feet, he crossed and crossed again their hiding ground, and more than one of the silent little sufferers he trampled to death, and neither knew nor cared.

Redruff had taken the yellow brute away off down-stream, and now returned to where he left his mate. The murderer had gone, taking her remains, to be thrown to the dog. Redruff sought about and found the bloody spot with feathers, Brownie's feathers, scattered around, and now he knew the meaning of that shot.

Who can tell what his horror and his mourning were? The outward signs were few, some minutes dumbly gazing at the place with downcast, draggled look, and then a change at the thought of their helpless brood. Back to the hiding-place he went, and called the well-known '*Kreet, kreet.*' Did every grave give up its little inmate at the magic word? No, barely more than half; six little balls of down unveiled their lustrous eyes, and, rising, ran to meet him, but four feathered little bodies had found their graves indeed. Redruff called again and again, till he was sure that all who could respond had come, then led them from that dreadful place, far, far away up-stream, where barb-wire fences and bramble thickets were found to offer a less grateful, but more reliable, shelter.

Here the brood grew and were trained by their father just as his mother had trained him; though wider knowledge and experience gave him many advantages. He knew so well the country round and all the feeding-grounds, and how to meet the ills that harass partridge-life, that the summer passed and not a chick was lost. They grew and flourished, and when the Gunner Moon arrived they were a fine family of six grown-up grouse with Redruff, splendid in his gleaming copper feathers, at their head. He had ceased to drum during the summer after the loss of Brownie, but drumming is to the partridge what singing is to the lark; while it is his love-song, it is also an expression of exuberance born of health, and when the molt was over and September food and weather had renewed his splendid plumes and braced him up again, his spirits revived, and finding himself one day near the old log he mounted impulsively, and drummed again and again.

From that time he often drummed, while his children sat around, or one who showed his father's blood would mount some nearby stump or stone, and beat the air in the loud tattoo.

The black grapes and the Mad Moon now came on. But Redruff's brood were of a vigorous stock; their robust health meant robust wits, and though they got the craze, it passed within a week, and only three had flown away for good.

Redruff, with his remaining three, was living in the glen when the snow came. It was light, flaky snow, and as the weather was not very cold, the family squatted for the night under the low, flat boughs of a cedar-tree. But next day the storm continued, it grew colder, and the drifts piled up all day. At night, the snow-fall ceased, but the frost grew harder still, so Redruff, leading the family to a birch-tree above a deep drift, dived into the snow, and the others did the same. Then into the holes the wind blew the loose snow – their pure white bed-clothes, and thus tucked in they slept in comfort, for the snow is a warm wrap, and the air passes through it easily enough for breathing. Next morning each partridge found a solid wall of ice before him from his frozen breath, but easily turned to one side and rose on the wing at Redruff's morning 'Kreet, kreet, kwit.' (Come children, come children, fly.)

This was the first night for them in a snowdrift, though it was an old story to Redruff, and next night they merrily dived again into bed, and the north wind tucked them in as before. But a change of weather was brewing. The night wind veered to the east. A fall of heavy flakes gave place to sleet, and that to silver rain. The whole wide world was sheathed in ice, and when the grouse awoke to quit their beds, they found themselves sealed in with a great cruel sheet of edgeless ice.

The deeper snow was still quite soft, and Redruff bored his way to the top, but there the hard, white sheet defied his strength. Hammer and struggle as he might he could make no impression, and only bruised his wings and head. His life had been made up of keen joys and dull hardships, with frequent sudden desperate straits, but this seemed the hardest brunt of all, as the slow hours wore on and found him weakening with his struggles, but no nearer to freedom. He could hear the struggling of his family, too, or sometimes heard them calling to him for help with their long-drawn plaintive '*p-e-e-e-e-t-e, p-e-e-e-e-t-e.*'

They were hidden from many of their enemies, but not from the pangs of hunger, and when the night came down the weary prisoners, worn out with hunger and useless toil, grew quiet in despair. At first they had been afraid the fox would come and find them imprisoned there at his mercy, but as the second night went slowly by they no longer cared, and even wished he would come and break the crusted snow, and so give them at least a fighting chance for life.

But when the fox really did come padding over the frozen drift, the deep-laid love of life revived, and they crouched in utter stillness till he passed. The second day was one of driving storm. The north wind sent his snow-horses, hissing and careering over the white earth, tossing and curling their white manes and kicking up more snow as they dashed on. The long, hard grinding of the granular snow seemed to be thinning the snow-crust, for though far from dark below, it kept on growing lighter. Redruff had pecked and pecked at the under side all day, till his head ached and his bill was wearing blunt, but when the sun went down he seemed as far as ever from escape. The night passed like the others, except no fox went trotting overhead. In the morning he renewed his pecking, though now with scarcely any force, and the voices or struggles of the others were no more heard. As the daylight grew stronger he could see that his long efforts had made a brighter spot above him in the snow, and he continued feebly pecking. Outside, the storm-horses kept on trampling all day, the crust was really growing thin under their heels, and late that afternoon his bill went through into the open air. New life came with this gain, and he pecked away, till just before the sun went down he had made a hole that his head, his neck, and his ever-beautiful ruffs could pass. His great broad shoulders were too large, but he could now strike downward, which gave him fourfold force; the snow-crust crumbled quickly, and in a little while he sprang from his icy prison once more free. But the young ones! Redruff flew to the nearest bank, hastily gathered a few red hips to stay his gnawing hunger, then returned to the prison-drift and clucked and stamped. He got only one reply, a feeble '*Peete, peete*,' and scratching with his sharp claws on the thinned granular sheet he soon broke through, and Graytail feebly crawled out of the hole. But that was all; the others, scattered he could not tell where in the drift, made no reply, gave no sign of life, and he was forced to leave them. When the snow melted in the spring their bodies came to view, skin, bones, and feathers – nothing more.

VII

It was long before Redruff and Graytail fully recovered, but food and rest in plenty are sure cure-alls, and a bright clear day in midwinter had the usual effect of setting the vigorous Redruff to drumming on the log. Was it the drumming, or the tell-tale tracks of their snow-shoes on the omnipresent snow, that betrayed them to Cuddy? He came prowling again and again up the ravine, with dog and gun, intent to hunt the partridges down. They knew him of old, and he was coming now to know them well. That great copper-ruffed cock was becoming famous up and down the valley. During the Gunner Moon many a one had tried to end his splendid life, just as a worthless wretch of old sought fame by burning the Ephesian wonder of the world. But Redruff was deep in wood-craft. He knew just where to hide, and when to rise on silent wing, and when to squat till overstepped, then rise on thunder wing within a yard to shield himself at once behind some mighty tree-trunk and speed away.

But Cuddy never ceased to follow with his gun that red-ruffed cock; many a long snapshot he tried, but somehow always found a tree, a bank, or some safe shield between, and Redruff lived and throve and drummed.

When the Snow Moon came he moved with Graytail to the Castle Frank woods, where food was plenty as well as grand old trees. There was in particular, on the east slope among the creeping hemlocks, a splendid pine. It was six feet through, and its first branches began at the tops of the other trees. Its top in summer-time was a famous resort for the bluejay and his bride. Here, far beyond the reach of shot, in warm spring days the jay would sing and dance before his mate, spread his bright blue plumes and warble the sweetest fairyland music, so sweet and soft that few hear it but the one for whom it is meant, and books know nothing at all about it.

This great pine had an especial interest for Redruff, now living near with his remaining young one, but its base, not its far-away crown, concerned him. All around were low, creeping hemlocks, and among them the partridge-vine and the wintergreen grew, and the sweet black acorns could be scratched from under the snow. There was no better feeding-ground, for when that insatiable gunner came on them there it was easy to run low among the hemlock to the great pine, then rise with a derisive *whirr* behind its bulk, and keeping the huge trunk in line with the deadly gun, skim off in safety. A dozen times at least the pine had saved them during the lawful murder season, and here it was that Cuddy, knowing their feeding habits, laid a new trap. Under the bank he sneaked and watched in ambush while an accomplice went around the Sugar Loaf to drive the birds. He came trampling through the low thicket where Redruff and Graytail were feeding, and long before the gunner was dangerously near Redruff gave a low warning '*rrr-rrr*' (danger) and walked quickly toward the great pine in case they had to rise.

Graytail was some distance up the hill, and suddenly caught sight of a new foe close at hand, the yellow cur, coming right on. Redruff, much farther off, could not see him for the bushes, and Graytail became greatly alarmed.

'*Kwit, kwit*' (Fly, fly), she cried, running down the hill for a start. '*Kreet, k-r-r-r*' (This way, hide), cried the cooler Redruff, for he saw that now the man with the gun was getting in range. He gained the great trunk, and behind it, as he paused a moment to call earnestly to Graytail, 'This way, this way,' he heard a slight noise under the bank before him that betrayed the ambush, then there was a terrified cry from Graytail as the dog sprang at her, she rose in air and skimmed behind the shielding trunk, away from the gunner in the open, right into the power of the miserable wretch under the bank.

Whirr, and up she went, a beautiful, sentient, noble being.

Bang, and down she fell – battered and bleeding, to gasp her life out and to lie, mere carrion in the snow.

It was a perilous place for Redruff. There was no chance for a safe rise, so he squatted low. The dog came within ten feet of him, and the stranger, coming across to Cuddy, passed at five feet, but he never moved till a chance came to slip behind the great trunk away from both. Then he safely rose and flew to the lonely glen by Taylor's Hill.

One by one the deadly cruel gun had stricken his near ones down, till now, once more, he was alone. The Snow Moon slowly passed with many a narrow escape, and Redruff, now known to be the only survivor of his kind, was relentlessly pursued, and grew wilder every day.

It seemed, at length, a waste of time to follow him with a gun, so when the snow was deepest, and food scarcest, Cuddy hatched a new plot. Right across the feeding-ground, almost the only good one now in the Stormy Moon, he set a row of snares. A cottontail rabbit, an old friend, cut several of these with his sharp teeth, but some remained, and Redruff, watching a far-off speck that might turn out a hawk, trod right in one of them, and in an instant was jerked into the air to dangle by one foot.

Have the wild things no moral or legal rights? What right has man to inflict such long and fearful agony on a fellow-creature, simply because that creature does not speak his language? All that day, with growing, racking pains, poor Redruff hung and beat his great, strong wings in helpless struggles to be free. All day, all night, with growing torture, until he only longed for death. But no one came. The morning broke, the day wore on, and still he hung there, slowly dying; his very strength a curse. The second night crawled slowly down, and when, in the dawdling hours of darkness, a great Horned Owl, drawn by the feeble flutter of a dying wing, cut short the pain, the deed was wholly kind.

The wind blew down the valley from the north. The snow-horses went racing over the wrinkled ice, over the Don Flats, and over the marsh toward the lake, white, for they were driven snow, but on them, scattered dark, were riding plumy fragments of partridge ruffs – the famous rainbow ruffs. And they rode on the winter wind that night, away and away to the south, over the dark and boisterous lake, as they rode in the gloom of his Mad Moon flight, riding and riding on till they were engulfed, the last trace of the last of the Don Valley race.

For now no partridge comes to Castle Frank. Its woodbirds miss the martial spring salute, and in Mud Creek Ravine the old pine drum-log, since unused, has rotted in silence away.

Luck of Life

◄O►

FRANCIS DICKIE

Francis Dickie (b. 1890) is a Canadian whose Scottish parents settled in Manitoba before the coming of the railway in 1880. Like many other writers of animal stories, he had a chequered career, having worked as a surveyor, logger and police reporter. He began writing in 1913, producing three novels and more than one hundred and fifty stories.

Umingmuk of the Barrens *(1927) (published also under the title* Monarch of the Prairies: The Life and Adventures of Umingmuk of the Barrens *[1933]), is an animal biography organized according to the pattern of an archetypal hero tale. The time is 1911, the place the Barrens of the Northwest Territories, where the musk-ox is born in June, "the one perfect month in all the year on these wonderful Arctic prairies." When Umingmuk's mother, his twin brother and the rest of the herd are captured by a big game hunter, Buffalo Smith, the musk-ox calf is left to survive on his own. The superior skills of the mythic hero – courage, strength, speed, determination, intelligence, curiosity – enable him to meet a variety of challenges until the climactic adventure described in "Luck of Life" establishes him as "King of the lonely Barren."*

Umingmuk, "the bearded one," is the Inuit name for these ancient animals which crossed to North America from Siberia about 90,000 years ago. In the nineteenth century, musk-oxen were seriously over-hunted to provide fresh meat for Inuit, Indians, foreign explorers and whalers, as well as to provide sleigh robes. In 1917 the Canadian government made them a protected species. Nowadays Inuit communities, hunting under a quota system, use the animals commercially. From the inner wool (qiviut), as fine and warm as cashmere, mittens, headbands, and sweaters are manufactured. An Inuvialuit food company will provide recipes for such gourmet dishes as "rib eye of Arctic muskox with maple sauce" and "medallions of Arctic muskox with Roquefort cheese and port wine sauce." Dickie's animal biography, though presented as fiction, gives an accurate representation of musk-oxen behaviour and of the harsh environment in which the animals thrive.

◄○►

Through the long winter Umingmuk added weight and height and length till his body reached maturity. When June looked once more upon the Barrens he was the finest of the herd, by Nature crowned with all the attributes of kingship. Ninety-four inches he was in length from the end of his nose to the tip of his two-inch tail. From his foreleg heel to his hump was sixty inches, and six hundred and five pounds was the weight of his body. His horns reached four inches beyond his eyes, a total sweep of thirty inches, while the bases were already near to meeting at the middle line. Such was Umingmuk in the third year of his life, a musk-ox commanding, because of his superior weight and height, for few herds contain animals with a body length of eight feet, a height of over five, and horns measuring two feet and a half.

He walked arrogantly now among the animals which he had the previous summer joined so meekly and gladly. The summer waxed to its hottest days of mid-July. Hotter it was than the previous year. The scarcely setting sun dried the old caribou moss into a brittle carpet dry as shavings, and even parched the vigorous new growth, hardy as it was to maintain life in this land of great extremes of heat and cold. No rain fell. Dry week followed dry week, till the tiny sloughs and even larger shallow lakes in the vicinity evaporated, forcing the herd to turn to the river for their supply.

But the banks of the Coppermine here sheered steeply for miles; the river had cut deeply into the surrounding plain. Only after much searching did the herd find a place where it was possible to reach the water, a little defile where now a dry streamlet's bed gave steeply upon the river. Even this was so narrow and so sharp of incline that only three of the herd could drink at one time, and then only at great inconvenience, for the swift river in cutting down through the plain now left the water level nearly two feet below that point where the streamlet emptied in early spring. Thus the musk-oxen had to go down on their knees on the creek bed that inclined steeply and stretch their necks far over the incline's end in order to touch the surface of the river. Still they would have continued frequenting this difficult spot had not one of the last year's calves overreached itself and gone slipping and sliding over the edge into the water and been whirled away, bawling despairingly, down the stream, the towering steep banks of which denied it a chance of ever gaining shore. The horror of the happening lay so heavy upon the herd that it went migrating in search of a new watering-place. The trek was, however, not alone due to the calf's misfortune, though this accident forced the herd sooner to a moving that would undoubtedly have eventually been made. The second reason was the animals' desire for shallow water where they could wallow and gain relief from the heat of summer.

Led by the old bulls, the animals, now increased to eighty head by the year's yield of calves, turned inland. Guided by some sixth sense, which in some beasts seems to detect water at a great distance, they came, at the end of the second day's march, upon a narrow lake about a mile long. To the east of its end was a splendid feeding-ground. In the new region the herd took up life again, spending long hours lying lolling in the shallow water, their bodies submerged, only their heads above the surface. At night they slept on the deep-mossed Barren to the east of the lake.

With the hot weather unusually prolonged this new lake was a very paradise to the heavy-furred creatures.

The sun on July's last day went down an unreal disk, its unusual draperies of red clouds and gold overlaid by a murky yellow. The Barren sunk to shadow and grew grey under a premature darkness. The usual hanging hush, that stillness so soundless it has a singing sounding all its own, strange paradox of the Barrens, was deeper this evening; more profound, as if in awe-some listening for a threatening terror tensely felt, anticipated, though unknown.

Uneasy the herd lay down, disquieted, in a saucer-like depression on the Barren about a mile from the end of the lake, for the grazing in the immediate vicinity of the water had been pretty well cropped of the choicest growth, and with plenty of feeding-ground the musk-oxen had become Arctic epicures.

As the night closed around them their restlessness increased. All were uneasy, from the oldest bull to the youngest calf, sensing something subtle of disaster in the brooding darkness and the silence more sombre than any night before.

Then out of the west, along the rim of the world where the sun had slipped over fully four hours past, once again light came breaking, long-flaring, and frightening with its sinister flaming, a brilliant dawning at a wrong point of earth. Rapidly it ran along the horizon, and came rushing eastward with comet-like speeding. The darkness fled before it across the Barren. The sleeping wilderness glowed with brightness unreal and eerie, and the silence was shattered by muffled roaring with a leitmotiv of sharper cracklings as of a million million toy guns simultaneously snapping; a wild refrain of destruction.

Ahead of the long red line fleeing came the routed battalions of the Barrens' army of animal life. First flew many great owls of the Arctic, strong pinioned and swift, their brown eyes no longer piti-lessly flashing, but dazed with the dread of this enemy advancing that knew no tiring; no stopping to rest. Close in their wake, many almost ready to fall from exhaustion, but still spurred on by fear of what followed, came scores of Arctic hares, gaunt-limbed racers, dun-hued masters of speed. Like long-legged ghosts in the unearthly brightness they flitted on and on, eyes ghastly, despairing; creatures maddened with fright. And racing with mile-devouring speed, stride famous in song and legend, came the pirates of the Barrens, the grey wolves, no longer terrible to every-thing that walked, but as craven as the rabbits, fear-filled with a panic that transcends all others. By ones and twos and half-dozens they sped along, spurning the miles behind them with frantic feet made doubly fleet by terror.

Up sprang the musk-oxen, after long hours of disquiet, now conscious of a danger subtly sensed but at first unknown. One moment quivering, each beast stood staring at the once black horizon now changed to a line of ever-nearing red, and then all got into motion, went galloping headlong over the tundra.

Quickly the glow grew all around them, till from horizon to zenith the sky behind them was aglare with the blaze of the on-rushing fire, an untiring runner that fast overtook all fleeing before it, save those on wings.

Well in front of the herd went Umingmuk, speeding, speeding. An hour passed. His breath, at first coming so easily, grew shorter. His saliva became cotton in his mouth and foamed white around his lips. A pain in his side from faint ache grew to an agony intol-erable. His forward movement, spurning at first the tundra with twenty-five-mile-an-hour gait, slackened imperceptibly, though he still exerted himself to the utmost, dashing on with sobbing breath and labouring sides, the night filled with his wheezing that was repeated by a dozen of his companions who still kept close behind him.

Another hour past, and now Umingmuk's run was slow almost as a trot. His following had dwindled to nine close companions. At various distances behind him, far scattered and straggling pitifully, the old ones of the herd moved heavily, the exhausted gaping calves deserted, left to the flames, fire-fear a greater thing than even mother-love.

Umingmuk's lungs were as an aching void scorched by shrivelling heat, and his head hung low as he hurried with the slowing steps of approaching exhaustion. Still on he went, bobbing along with queer musk-oxen gait like a toy rocking-horse violently agitated on a semicircular base.

With the beginning of the third hour of the flight, close came the flame on his heels. The world all about him was brilliantly alight from the blaze of the Barren where the thick carpet of the dead moss of many previous years lay brown, brittle and dry, a perfect fuel that fed the flames and gave them monstrous speed, unslackening, inexorable, against which no beast that ever trod the tundra had a chance by flight.

Of all the panics which living things – men, beasts and birds – are heir to, that born of fire is the greatest; no others even nearly compare in power. Fire-fear robs many of mankind, and all the animal kingdom, of reason's every vestige. Otherwise, Umingmuk and his kind, while there had been yet time, instead of starting off ahead of the flame, would have dashed back and soaked themselves to the shoulder in the water of the lake. Of course, even here death might have come to them by suffocation by the smoke that lies close and heavy over such surfaces when fire is near. Still, the lake offered at least a chance for life. Now the animals had none. But that first sight of the flaming heavens had turned them all into mere mechanisms that madly moved. Blind terror was their portion. Even the sense of direction became sunk in the general numbness, so that Umingmuk, in the second hour of his flight, had unconsciously swung farther and farther to the left until at last, instead of racing ahead of the flames, he was moving on a line parallel with the advancing fire, an occurrence which, unbelievable as it may seem, is quite common among animals of widely different kinds when driven before a far-reaching line of fire on prairie or in forest, as has been beyond doubt established by the observation of men similarly fleeing, but not so robbed of mind as to be unnoticing of so strange a happening.

With the fire still some distance behind him, Umingmuk continued this parallel course, and the nine musk-oxen closest had followed.

Moving on ever slower, Umingmuk went, while the fire maintained a speed unchanging. The wall of flame, distant by a mile the first hour of the hegira, cut down the intervening space by more than half in the second. By the middle of the third hour only a hundred yards separated Umingmuk and his companions from the racing, roaring furnace.

Frenzied, blundering on despairful, staggering in strides that were painful, and more demanding on his fading strength as the minutes flew, yet producing only lope that was laggard and losing compared with the pace of the fire, Umingmuk went forward upon his parallel way. The flames grew closer. Seventy yards only lay between him and death's scorching breath. The distance narrowed to fifty; then thirty. Yet all his concentrated effort produced less speed than what he could have made at a canter on an ordinary occasion. The air he gasped in now was fiery, and doubly seared lungs, already for long painful, seemed molten. He stumbled, fell; rose only by terrific effort; ran on. Suddenly the air came cooler to his nostrils; less smoke-filled, purer. Yet half a dozen lengths and down again he came. This time he recovered his feet more slowly than the last; ran hobblingly; fell again within a dozen yards; rose. Three hundred yards perhaps he made before he fell a fourth time, and lay still, run to exhaustion.

Yet no consuming flames swept over his prostrate form, for luck of life was his and those few of his kind who had been able to keep near him.

Luck of life? – Yes; luck of life! – one term fit, and one term only, by which to explain Umingmuk's salvation and that of his few companions; that in his panic fleeing he should have taken a course which, ordinarily, would have meant destruction only the quicker in its coming; but instead had been the means of his retaining life and leading to safety the instinctively following few of the herd whose speed had been sufficiently lasting to keep near to him, by Nature given such superior virility. Had Umingmuk gone to the right, instead of to the left, a jump into the Coppermine ultimately would have faced him, had he succeeded in outrunning the fire to the water's edge; this a mere changing of the form of death from burning to drowning after a dread voyage on the bosom of a swift and treacherous-currented river whose steep banks would have kept him to the water till death overtook him.

But running to the left, parallel with the advancing fire, he had outrun it; passed beyond the end of the wall of flame, which had been diverted by a narrow stretch of Barren where half a dozen flat rocks close together protruded slab-like faces, a few inches above the surface. These slabs of rock covered scarcely two hundred square feet; they were bare of any growth, and had sent the fire swerving around them to the right.

No more freakish element of destruction exists than fires of great magnitude which sweep through large forests or over vast expanses of prairie or Barren. The slightest obstacle often suffices to deflect the course of such conflagrations, and the flames, swept onward by the terrific wind of their own creating, will actually break off short at certain points and leave untouched a stretch of territory covered with inflammable matter.

Such had happened to the flame in Umingmuk's rear. Swerved by the rock, the fire-line had swept eastward, the deflection leaving untouched a strip of Barren on which Umingmuk and his companions found safety.

The thin smoke lying over Umingmuk presently cleared, drawn southward by the draught of the heavier rolling masses. Still breathing with considerable effort, his throat parched and paining, Umingmuk got heavily to his feet. A weariness beyond words, such as never before had he even nearly approached, lay upon him. The sound of hoarse, drawn breath now caught his ears. Turning, he saw, ten yards behind him, a yearling cow lying on her side, her flanks heaving. Beyond her a few feet another young cow was just in the act of arising, while scattered beyond her again over a hundred yards of area lay seven others of the band in various sprawling positions of rest, all still too weak to arise. Umingmuk saw with surprise that all were young cows. Neither of the old or young bulls had escaped. Umingmuk's eyes moved to the racing destruction now far ahead and to the right, the clouds of yellow-white smoke partially obscuring the flame. The short night was over. Day was upon the land, though the smoke rolling heavenward blotted out the sun.

For several moments Umingmuk stood gazing upon the desolation before him and at these few exhausted members of a once fine herd. Presently something of the natural leadership that was his by virtue of his sex and size moved him to action. He walked over to where the first cow lay flat, and nuzzled her encouragingly till she made an effort and succeeded in rising. In turn he roused the rest of the survivors, gathered them together.

The country was strange. Yet to Umingmuk, with the nine young cows beside him, there came a sudden vast assurance, the poise and calmness and air of command natural to one destined for leadership. Proudly he raised his head. Then, though still very weary, he went across the level Barren to the northward through the land left untouched by fire, his nostrils scenting for water, upon the finding of which now so much depended. And, recognizing his leadership, the nine cows came close at his heels, made confident by Umingmuk's lordly bearing, his immediate assumption of command.

Long and hard was the march, and nearly done was even Umingmuk when that seeming sixth sense, so strong in some creatures of the wild, brought him at last late on the following day to a new lake about a mile in length. The surrounding country was a rich pasture land.

Here in this new domain, with his nine followers so obedient and admiring, Umingmuk came into the kingship for which he had been fitted with fine body and fleetness by wise Mother Nature. And here, far from his place of birth, he reigned among an admiring and obedient following, King of the lonely Barren, sole monarch of this wilderness stretch.

Belette the Weasel

◄O►

DONALD G. DODDS

Donald G. Dodds (b.1925) wrote Wild Captives *(1965), from
which "Belette the Weasel" comes, during the winter of 1957-8
while the author was a wildlife biologist employed by the government of Newfoundland. The stories were written in the evening by
the light of a kerosene lamp – "partly for relaxation and partly to
gain some perspective of the research problems I was dealing
with." Subsequently, Dodds was Professor of wildlife biology at
Acadia University in Wolfville, Nova Scotia.*

The purpose of Wild Captives *was to depict accurately, without
sentimentality, the lives of various wild animals commonly found in
the Canadian wilderness – lynx, hare, moose, weasel, fox, marten,
caribou, wolf, wolverine, bear – and to convey the impact that*

human intervention has on animal population. "All animals are in reality captives of mankind," says Dodds. "I hope this book shows how quickly an animal's freedom can be turned into death because of man's presence."

The well-developed senses that equip naturalists to observe animal life also make them keenly aware of habitat. Dodds evokes the beauty and mystery of the forest through the seasonal cycle which controls the weasel's activities. The violence necessary to survival is presented in a straightforward manner that makes us admire the animal's efficient use of its physical attributes: "Belette crunches the mouse's head, his needle teeth piercing the skull, and feeds." The author reiterates Charles G.D. Roberts' attitude to nature "red in tooth and claw" – the individual dies but the species survives "by the grace of many miracles."

◄o►

The snow and the night have changed the face of the forest. Frothy white cones reach for the stars and the high, bright moon. Early that day the forest was green, but snow fell during the hours of light, stopping at dusk, and now the clear, white night is new.

In the dense fir, chickadees roost, brown caps and black caps together. Crossbills, jays, and grosbeaks sleep under the limbs and snow. In the morning, when the four-footed animals seek a sheltered rest, birds will emerge to greet the dawn and feed. If they slept till dawn was full and past, they would be safe from the predator, but this they cannot do.

A fox calls, his beautiful, mournful cry repeated. The dog seeks a mate this February night. As if in answer, the echo sounds. Then another fox takes up the cry and there are four.

Beside a fallen birch the snow stirs. It rises slightly a few inches on one side of the quilted log, and then the magic is repeated on the other side. Suddenly the snow explodes at the base of the upturned stump. A ghost-white Belette sits up, sniffing the frosted night. The moonlight, feeling its way between the giant boughs, picks out the black-bead eyes and, against the snow cushion, the black tip of a shivering tail. Belette moves into the beam of light and faces the moon. It is very bright to his eyes but he sits motion-less for several minutes.

A great white owl sails over the tree-tips near by. It swoops into the forest and perches on a crooked, snow-covered crag of birch. The owl does not hear or see the weasel, for Belette has not moved. Once covered by the bird's shadow, he waits before making the movement that might reveal his presence to the ears and eyes of the owl.

Belette sits peering straight at the moon, paws slanting down-wards against his stomach. Then, in one quick movement, he is hidden by snow-cover, silent and still beneath the blanket. The owl senses no movement. No sound is audible, even to the great drum ears inside the feathered head.

One of the foxes in the moonlight comes padding through the fluff. Beneath the owl tree he stops and looks up. He moves his head about, cocking it to one side, and sits down to examine the

white bird outlined against the sky. Only the head of the owl moves to watch the fox. Vulpes frisks about, tired of watching. He dives into the snow, head first, front paws digging swiftly. Small snow clouds flurry and settle in pieces on the tail and back of the fox. Vulpes looks up from his white cave towards the owl with a snow-covered face, and burrows again.

Belette must move now. The fox is very close. There is a purpose to the game. Quickly Belette slithers through the snow to the mouse-tunnels below and at once is gone. Vulpes digs, listens, smells, and digs. There is more than one odour here. The weasel has escaped, but where the weasel is there also may be mice.

Through the fluff to the old snow crust he digs – through the crust to the granules beneath. A movement under his paws stirs Vulpes to dig faster, leap high in the air – straight up, and down – then snap and drop the furry fluff. Vulpes holds his nose almost against the mouse, a paw resting at either side. The mouse sits up, pawing at the giant. Its teeth show and the mouth moves open and shut. Vulpes picks the mouse up gently. His lips are curled and only his incisors grip the prey. Snapping his neck back, he throws the mouse behind him into the fluffy snow. Quickly the fox jumps up, and down again at the mouse. The squeal is heard by the owl who swerves down from his perch, sailing close to Vulpes' back. The fox turns and snaps at the passing bird, looks down, and delicately chews off the digestive tract of his meal, to leave for the first morning jay.

Belette moves through the maze of tunnels, sometimes turning in his path to back-track a distance. Everywhere is the scent of mice. He crosses tiny midden heaps, fresh cut from rhizomes in the loose earth beneath the winter blanket. Mouse droppings are everywhere along the track-beaten maze. At a junction he surprises a resident moving across his path. The chase is short. Belette crunches the mouse's head, his needle teeth piercing the skull, and feeds.

It is late March. When the wind blows Belette's fur, brown shows beneath the white coat. Birds are becoming active, and the weasel, lying motionless beneath alder clumps, takes more of the flying creatures than during the time of winter's deadness.

April comes and Belette is greyish in colour, the brown hair casting shadows through the lingering white. Then May arrives and Belette is brown.

He travels farther now, even though food is plentiful. It is time to breed, and he seeks the sedentary female.

Gracilis moves out from her rock den high above the stream-bed. Over the clinging trunk roots turned quickly up by the sun and the earth, she moves over the ledge to the level ground above her. She is smaller by half than Belette. Narrower in the head and body, she is daintier, more fragile than the male, yet she disciplines her spring mate. For two weeks the weasels have shared the same den and the same food. Belette has brought small birds, beetles, and mice to the den. The animals chatter, purr, and sometimes bark. On occasion, Gracilis has found it necessary to nip Belette's ear to win her share.

Gracilis has hunted, too, but over a shorter distance and, over the days, with less success. Her needs are not as great as the male's. She is used to moving less, hunting less, eating less.

Now she moves beneath the fir stump on the ledge and out the opposite side, across the moss carpet to the big boulder, and is gone. Beneath this boulder is a den Gracilis has often known. The entrance is an opening in the moss carpet made by the near-surface root growth of a spruce tree, appearing only as a crack in the ground. Scurrying around through the fissures created by the struggling young soil over the boulder's edge, she searches for any living thing, for food. Now, out she pops and scurries outside the tree-cover into the young grass near the old abandoned camp. Soon, there will be a host of grasshoppers here, but now she passes through the grass to the camp and the many beetles.

Belette is stirred by his mate's return. The female acts differently. She shoves her head beneath Belette's and chuckles. Belette grasps the female's neck harshly, making Gracilis bark and screech. The mating begins. It is June the tenth.

The young will not be born until the following spring, for development of the now-fertile eggs will be retarded until late the following winter. The mating over, Belette will begin to stray farther from the female's home range until his movements bring him back infrequently. But in the spring, if he survives, he may return.

Mid-July finds the many young weasels born that spring exploring the outside world for the first time. Behind their mother they scamper over and under, searching out food. Throughout the summer and fall, many are caught by birds of prey and foxes. Some are drowned attempting to cross the too-swift streams. A few die from disease.

Belette seeks out the carrion and waste about the campgrounds this summer. He feeds on discarded meat, taking fly and beetle larvae eagerly with the carrion. There are also plenty of grasshoppers and young birds, and Belette grows fat. In winter, exposure to the cold above snow-cover quickly destroys a weasel careless enough to rest outside. With fat and full stomach, the fall weasel is hardier than the late winter animal.

Weasels, too, can grow lazy. The easy life about the camp prompts Belette to go on living the same way. In September, when the wind ruffles his brown fur to show the approaching white coat beneath, Belette begins a journey to the farm.

By January the white hunter has destroyed all the rats and mice from the woodshed, but there is always garbage behind the building.

Today the smell of fresh meat lures Belette to the barn. Inside hang the dripping quarters of moose. On the floor the blood puddles emit a heavy odour. Belette darts straight to the warm liquid. There is movement near him but he is fearless. It is the cat who has been given credit for Belette's hunting successes, and now Belette himself is killed. It will be unfortunate for the cat if another weasel does not now arrive to do the feline's work for him.

Back in her rock den, Gracilis lies curled, a tiny ball of deadly life, her head hidden by a stomach and tail. Within her, six minute specks will become three male and three female weasels by spring, by the grace of many miracles.

The Waif of
Prairie Hollows

◄○►

H. MORTIMER BATTEN

H. Mortimer Batten (1889-1958) was born in England, trained as an engineer and served as a despatch rider for the French army during World War I (receiving the Croix de Guerre). He was also an inventor, test driver, wildlife photographer, BBC broadcaster, storyteller, magistrate of a Scottish island and prolific author. As a member of a geological survey team in 1912-13, he became familiar with the Canadian north. Forty years later, in 1953, he visited Lac Le Jeune, near Kamloops, British Columbia, for a three-day fishing trip and stayed for the rest of his life. This proved to be one of his most productive periods, resulting in two collections of animal stories, Whispers of the Wilderness: Tales of Wild Life in the Canadian Forests *(1960) and* Wild and Free: Stories of

Canadian Animals *(1961) as well as numerous articles, many illus-
trated with his own photographs, that were published in*
Blackwood's Magazine, Scottish Field, Country Life, Rod and
Gun *and elsewhere.*

*"The Waif of Prairie Hollows" belongs to an earlier period,
having been published originally in* Romances of the Wild *(1922),
a fact that accounts for some strange and dated terminology. Set in
the foothills country of Alberta, the story bears some resemblance
to "The Springfield Fox" by Ernest Thompson Seton, whose
concept of animal heroes greatly influenced Batten's development
of the realistic animal story. Another point of similarity is their
expertise in identifying animal tracks. Batten's* Wild Animals and
Their Tracks *was adopted as an official publication by the Boy
Scouts, an association which Seton claimed to have inspired.
Other books by Mortimer Batten include* Dramas of the Wild Folk
(1924), The Golden Book of Animal Stories *(1927) and* The
Singing Forest *(1955).*

◄O►

That dawn Strychnine Loam, returning across the prairie from a
carousal in town, saw a jackal skulking along the north bank
of the Silvertrail and shot it at surprisingly long range. Pelts were of
little value at this season, mid-spring, but bounties were good –
especially for *she* wolves and jackals. When Loam rode up to his
prize he was at first gratified, then angry – gratified to find it was a
she jackal, and angry to discover that she was nursing little ones.

The wolfer had no humane sentiments in the matter – oh, no. To him a wolf or a jackal merely represented a bounty, and whereas this blunder of his meant a death of lingering misery to the coyote's cubs, what really concerned him was that he had cheated himself out of the possession of the whole litter. Had he known that the coyote was nursing whelps he would have waited in hiding for her, armed with a light rifle, and given her a flesh wound that would maim but not kill. Then the coyote, feeling the great sickness upon her, would have crept to her cubs, leaving behind her a betraying blood trail, and the wolfer, exultant, could have tracked her to her den, where seven or eight bounties, in addition to that for the mother, would have been his.

Two days later young Steth Elwood, the son of the range owner, accompanied by the ranch boss, Lee, was riding along the Silvertrail when, turning suddenly, he was surprised to see what he took to be a puppy scrambling over the ground on clumsy legs in pursuit of Queenie, the fox terrier, who accompanied them.

"Well, look at that, Lee!" cried Steth. "Where did that little beggar spring from?"

Lee looked, and as they both drew rein Queenie turned upon the puppy with a snarl, whereupon the little creature rolled over in an attitude of surrender, and Queenie was disarmed. Her heart was soft, for at home she had puppies of her own, but as she trotted on the little animal followed, and the men saw it was so weak as to be scarcely able to stand.

"Hold on," said Lee. "It's a little coyote. You ride south there and head him off."

The coyote whelp, however, was so absorbed in following the terrier that it took not the least notice of the men, so that the task of catching it was by no means the exciting business they had expected. Lee slipped from his saddle and called Queenie; then, as the puppy came ambling up, looking at the man curiously, Steth threw his rope from behind, and the coyote was a captive.

It is to be feared that he bit and squealed and made Lee's thumb bleed, at which the ranch boss was all for tapping the little captive across the scalp and drawing the bounty.

"No," said Steth, "we'll take him home."

Lee looked at the boy. Like all cattle-punchers, he regarded coyotes much as one might regard a steel trap that possessed legs and ran about the range trapping anything of value to man.

"What on earth for?" he inquired. "Jackals ain't no good as pets, and I bet the boss will kick if you take him home."

"I can do as I like," retorted Steth, with an importance of a person inspired by seventeen summers. "And – look here, Lee! If we put that cub in a box having an open front, his mother will come and feed him, and then we can get her, too – you savvy?"

Lee grinned.

"She'll come and gnaw him out!" the man prophesied. Then, after a moment's thought, he added: "Anyway, we can try it, Master Steth. I've got a couple of number-three traps somewhere about the outfit, and we'll go shares in the bounty."

So the baby coyote was taken back to the ranch, given some milk, and finally placed in a chicken-coop at the back of the outhouses. Steth and Lee decided not to place any traps till the mother had been once or twice, and so had overcome her natural suspicion of this close proximity of man, so round the coop they spread some wire netting to prevent her gnawing him out.

The little coyote cried all night, as he had cried with his brothers and sisters all the previous night, but his mother never came, because she was dead. There was only one who heard and understood his plaintive whimperings – Queenie, the terrier; and somehow it made her restless, rising constantly to turn round and lick her own puppies. Once the coyote thought he got a faint whiff of his mother, and his cries went up in a wild crescendo. He did not yet know the scent of the timber wolf as he came to know it later, and the wolf, fearing some trap, decided not to go right in and kill that wretched little coyote.

Next morning Steth was surprised to find that the mother had not been near, so he fed the little captive and left everything as before. The cookee noticed that Queenie visited the coop several times during the day, and on her last visit her suspicion of the cub seemed to have died a natural death, for she was seen to lick his nose through the bars.

That evening, when Queenie was out with her master, one of the men went with a bucket of water and did something dreadful to Queenie's puppies. They were all mongrels, you see, and the regular arrival of Queenie's families necessitated steps of this sort. So, when Queenie hastened back to her brood, she found her nest empty, save for the scent of the murderer's hands.

She searched high and low, miserably unhappy, and at the back of her mind was a lurking suspicion that man had done this thing. Had she possessed the faintest inkling of it she would have hidden the puppies in that secret cache of hers, behind the stick heap, where she hid so many of her treasures; and now, having searched the buildings, she went down to the Silvertrail, and her mother sense took her to a little patch of newly turned sand. Here she found her little ones buried – cold, stiff, no longer a joy to her loving eyes, and she stole away from the horrible place, fearful of being seen in her misery, and hid in the stick heap.

That night the captive coyote whimpered, and Queenie listened. The sound stirred and kindled the mother love within her, and when all was quiet she stole out from her hiding and went to the coop. Wire nettings and the taint of man had no fears for her, and, forcing her way through the barrier, she gnawed the puppy free.

Deep in the stick pile Queenie hid him, and there for many days the little fosterling rejoiced in undivided possession of the food that was meant for seven. He throve apace, and his dread of man grew in proportion. Only at night-time did he venture from the stick heap, to sit, with his big ears erect, his forelegs wide apart, cocking his head from side to side as he watched the buzzing moths and silly-bumbles.

As for Steth – he and his confederate arrived at the most natural conclusion. The only man along the range who could have distinguished the tracks of the terrier from those of a wild coyote was Strychnine Loam, the trapper, and him they did not take into their confidence. "She's been and taken him," was Steth's report, and when Lee had ambled up to look for himself his only comment was: "First time I've ever known a coyote to face wire netting."

Though the little coyote was growing rapidly in strength and staunchness of limb, his education was being sadly neglected. Had his mother lived she would, by this time, have taken him nightly on breathless mouse-hunting expeditions, and thus, lesson by lesson, he would have learned from her the things on which his success in after life was dependent. As it was he received no such training; but for a coyote he was gaining a good deal of unique experience.

A jackal is truly a creature of the wild. Keep him a captive all his life, force him into circus tricks if you like, but his fear and distrust of man will never die. Certain wiles of the chase the coyote knew by instinct, and example was not necessary in order to show him how to lurk in waiting among the sticks, then spring out at the sleek, grey rats that sometimes ventured within his domain. Sillybumbles he caught by the score, and one day the rat trick developed into a far more exciting and perilous pastime.

A great white partridge came and sat on the stick pile and sang in a most startling and raucous manner. Coyote had seen these partridges before and knew that they were good to eat, though he had feared to venture into the yard where they lived. Now he mounted noiselessly and leaped, and the rooster vanished into the stick pile with no knowledge as to the manner of death that had seized him from below.

That evening, when Queenie came to feed him, coyote was not hungry, and the next morning found him in the same state. This was because rats had been attracted to the stick pile by the remains of the chicken, and, observing this, coyote had used the remains as a bait – carrying it into an open spot where there was nothing to hinder his pounce.

During the next few days several chickens disappeared. The little jackal became self-supporting, and Queenie began to lose interest in him. One evening one of the boys, sauntering round the stick heap, saw white feathers everywhere.

"It's the rats in the stick heap what's taking them chickens!" he reported to Lee, and Lee got to work with a number of "small fur" traps, setting them as far back in the heap as convenience permitted. "That'll fix 'em!" was his final comment, and, sure enough, it fixed the little coyote within quite a few minutes. The trap closed on one of his forelegs, and at first he simply "kia-wooed" for Queenie, thinking that something had bitten him; but, finding himself held, the instinctive terror of the trapped animal fell upon him. Dead to all pain, he dragged the trap deep into the stick heap, and there, for ten hours, fought and wrestled with it in an agony of fear and pain. Queenie went to him, but he was so fierce and red-eyed that she dare not go near. More terrible than a wolf trap was the one he had encountered, for it had tearing, cruel teeth, whereas a wolf trap is blunt and toothless.

With the early dawn the little coyote freed himself from the dreadful thing, for after all it was only a "small fur" trap, and then it was that a great suspicion of this place fell upon him. He crept out of his hiding and, for the first time, looked with interest upon the world without. The red rim of the sun was just peeping over the endless haze of the prairies. Away to the west the foothills rolled in an unending succession of light and shadow, and farther still the great dim buttes reared like cloud palaces above the haze. It was an infinite world, endlessly beautiful, breathlessly grand, and into it stole little coyote, casting fearful glances behind him as he hopped on three legs and nursed a fourth.

He was leaving the ranch for ever, but with him he took this much knowledge – that safety from man is to be found in his very midst, and that the scent of steel is the scent of *death*.

Strychnine Loam, so named on account of his alleged skill with poisoned baits, had his cabin at the cañon mouth, about five miles from the ranch, and one day, returning home with a large catch of whitefish, he left them strung under the eaves of his cabin to dry out prior to curing them for baits. Returning home hours later, he had just cast off his gear when he found that his feet were entangled in something. It was the line by which he had left the fish suspended!

All the whitefish were gone, and there, up to the very threshold of his cabin, were the tracks of a coyote – so fresh that a beetle it had trodden upon was still alive in its uncrushed portion.

The jackal must have been here when Loam rode up, and his quick senses prompted him to look about him. Was that a jackal, or was it a clump of cactus, there in the sand not twenty paces away? The wolfer did not look straight in that direction, and now he began to whistle a careless air, engaging himself by disentangling his feet. But he caught a glimpse of one bright eye shining from the inconspicuous little mound, and knew that it was a jackal.

Not ten seconds ago Loam had laid his revolver on the bench inside the cabin, and now there was nothing for it but to go and get the weapon. With a natural swing he turned in at the door, took up the revolver, and stepped out ready to use it.

But the mound was gone! Yes, that second when his back was turned had given the animal the chance for which it was watching – the chance to put the cabin between itself and the man. Loam dodged to the back, just in time to see a little cyclone of dust heading straightaway – a young, gaunt-limbed coyote that ran on three legs and nursed a fourth!

Next day, when Loam went his round, he again left a string of baits suspended upon the wall, and beneath them, hidden in the sand, were two number-four Whitehouse traps. When he came

home at dusk one of the traps had been pulled out and sprung, and dirt was scratched upon the other. The baits were gone!

Strange that a coyote who had never mixed with his own kind since his helpless puppy days should grow up with all the little tricks that betray the coyotes the world over inherent in him. As a matter of fact, Lame Leg had narrowly escaped the wolfer's set, and this experience added one more stone to the temple of his knowledge – that suspended baits, though tempting, are dangerous.

A little while later Steth Elwood met the wolfer on the range.

"There's a blame little wise coyote that I can't trap about my cabin," said Loam. "Seen anything of him along at the ranch?"

The boy shook his head.

"No!" he answered; then after a moment's thought he added: "But hold on – one of the boys pegged out some skunk skins to dry. When he went in the morning something – a dog, we thought – had rolled on them and chewed up the best and finished by scattering dirt on them."

Loam laughed.

"That's a coyote trick, sure enough," said he. "Fairly reeks of coyote! What was your dog doing that she allowed him about?"

They both looked at Queenie.

"Dunno," said the boy. "She usually sends any coyote that happens along about his business, so I guess she must have been asleep."

But not even Queenie's master knew much about the night side of her character in these days – how, almost every evening, a little lame coyote would approach by the corral, thence through the stick heap, to meet her at the gate. A friendly sign would pass between them, then the coyote would trot around as though he owned the place. He would explore the garbage heap, sniff round the hen house, and trot off with anything left lying about. Once a pair of chaparajos, hanging on the bunk-house wall, were missing when morning came, but later one of them was found roughly buried in the dunghill.

All this time Lame Leg was collecting for himself a wonderful assortment of knowledge. The injury to his paw was, alas, permanent, and, deprived of his speed, he was compelled to rely more and more upon his wits. But for his intimacy with the haunts of man he would have fared badly in these days, for in many ways the injury was a serious menace to him. Wolves – the big, husky timber wolves – are to-day as plentiful in the Silvertrail valley as when the buffalo myriads moved north and south each spring and fall. The buffalo are gone with the coming of man, but in their place man has stocked the foothills richly with herds of cattle, sheep, and goats. On these the wolves feast, and between the wolves and the coyotes there exists a never-relenting feud. Lame Leg moved in mortal terror of the wolves, and it was only because they concluded that he was as fleet as the rest of his kind that he had managed to survive so long.

That fall young Elwood organized a series of wolf and coyote hunts, every dog in the locality being mustered to the meet, whereupon the scratch pack, with an equally scratch gathering of hunters, would beat the sage and the juniper for any lurking vermin. In spite of the undisciplined conduct of the pack, most of the members of which seemed to regard the meet simply as a matchmaking affair, a surprising number of coyotes were killed – coyotes which, possessing the hereditary weaknesses of their kind, could not resist the temptation of running to the crest of the ridges to see what all the canine excitement was about, then yap their mockery. Moreover, those that fell did so because they trusted to their fleetness and in the end were outdistanced.

Wolves, too, were killed – one or two long-legged cubs of that year – and so were a good many of the dogs. There was one wolf in particular that gave the pack trouble – a big, gaunt, black-maned brute, whom the boys knew as Buffalo. This wolf had long mocked the efforts of Strychnine Loam, and it was this wolf that finally broke up the pack – or, rather, broke up so many of its members that young Steth found himself in the midst of a seething indignation of bereaved dog-owners who demanded compensation.

"You'll have to take it in a sporting spirit," said young Steth. "I can't pay you for your dogs, since you've had your share of the fun, but I'll tell you what I'll do. That big wolf is doubtless at the bottom of all this cattle killing, and I'll supplement the bounty by one hundred dollars to be paid the man who gets him. Now vamoose!"

They vamoosed, but the only one who went his way with a sense of contentment was Strychnine Loam, the professional trapper of the range.

Just as there was one exceptional wolf upon the foothills, so there was one exceptional coyote – exceptional because he contrived to avoid the limelight. Other coyotes might stand in silhouette upon the hill-tops, yapping their mockery, but *he* did not. Other coyotes might depend upon their speed, but *he* had no speed and knew it. His strength lay in the knowledge of his own weakness, for on hearing the pack from afar he would sneak by the shadowy hollows away to the ranch – would hide in the very stick heap of his nursery days! No one thought of looking there; in fact, the hunt generally met two miles from the ranch and broke up an equal or a greater distance away. Only at night-time does the truly wild coyote come prowling round the habitation of man, and so, at man's very threshold, Lame Leg sought and found a sanctuary denied his abler kin.

Almost nightly Queenie saw her adopted son, and while there were no great demonstrations between them, each seemed content to regard the other as a natural feature of the landscape. Then one night when Lame Leg came he offered Queenie an invitation to come out with him in the most approved dog form. The invitation consisted of a nudge of the shoulder, then trotting briskly off he would look round at Queenie to follow. At first she was reluctant, for her duty lay at home, but three times he came back for her and in the end she yielded. Away up-wind he led her, across the prairie levels where the shadows lay like ghost-clouds, through gopher cities where the citizens sat like picket pins, then vanished backward into their burrows with "churrs" of derision as the two dogs trotted up. Once a great grey ghost-bird settled just ahead, and Lame Leg and Queenie dashed at it with chopping jaws.

The blood of the wild dog was astir in Queenie's veins, and as she trotted on her mane began to bristle and her eyes shone with the wild hunting lust. Dim and unreal the prairie lay ahead, a land of half-lights, of shifting shadows; just in front of her was her wolfish friend, and there was no sound in the vastness save the "pitter-pat" of their paws on the sand.

Suddenly Lame Leg stopped, his head aloft, sifting every breeze. A faint whiff came down the night air, faint but seductive – the delicious whiff of calf – and Queenie was for going right in here and now had not Lame Leg warned her with a growl. Up-wind he went, very cautiously, zigzagging, yard by yard, and Queenie, who knew nothing of the perils of the coyote world, wondered at his caution. Fifty paces, thirty, twenty; then, convinced the coast was clear, Lame Leg trotted up and they feasted.

Presently Lame Leg raised his head, growled, and stole away, motioning Queenie to follow. And as they went there stole from the darkness a huge black-maned wolf, who rumbled thunder as he came; and, seated on a near-by ridge, Lame Leg yapped his mockery while the wolf feasted, and Queenie looked on with shining eyes.

That was but the first of their nocturnal forays together, and soon it became the fashion for Lame Leg to invite his foster-mother to any feast he found, and for Queenie to accept.

Many dogs in wild regions adopt at nightfall the habits of the wolf, living all day with their masters till, at the coming of dusk, civilization falls from them like the falling of a veil, and they sneak up-wind, watchful, furtive, hiding from man should he appear upon the sky-line. And as sure as night follows day, as sure as the Snow Moon brings her snows, their wolfish habits, sooner or later, land them in dire straits.

One night, when the crisp evening chills had turned to deadly frosts, Queenie, passing a pine thicket with Lame Leg at her side, saw a prairie chicken hanging by its head from a bough about six feet from the ground. She looked up at it and whined to attract the coyote's attention, at which he rumbled a warning in his throat and barged her with his shoulder. But the prairie chicken smelt irresistibly good, and Queenie was reluctant to leave it, though her companion's growls and bristling mane forbade her touching it.

Next day Queenie remembered the prairie chicken. She thought Lame Leg had warned her against it because he wanted to return for it himself, and so she sneaked off alone to secure the prize.

Under the suspended bird, though perhaps a yard to the north of it, was an ant-hill, now a mound of snow, from the crest of which the bait hung within easy reach. Cautiously Queenie mounted the hillock, sniffing suspiciously, for she, too, had an inbred fear of traps. The crown of the mound was a likely place for a setting, but Queenie soon learned there was no trap there and climbed up eagerly, her eyes bright with the light of possession. There dangled the prairie chicken, within easy springing distance, moving tempt-ingly in the breeze. Queenie leaped and seized it, fell back to earth with the prize in her jaws, when – thud! The trap was hidden, not at the starting-point, but at the landing, and now Queenie was firmly held by the blunt, remorseless jaws of a number-four Whitehouse!

How she fought and screamed and tussled, while no sound came to her save the mockery of the echoes! Ere long the imprisoned paw was dead and cold; she was conscious of no pain save the mental agony of being trapped. She fell to gnawing the trap, the chain, the drag – gnawed at her own imprisoned paw below the jaws, but there was no escaping from that vise-like hold.

The day died in a sullen glory of crimson – night came, but, luckily for Queenie, the frost snap had relented somewhat. But night brought its manifold terrors and shifting shadows, and the little dog crouched lower now, flattened herself to earth, and lay still in silent dread.

One hour, two hours passed by, then just behind her Queenie heard a sound like a human sigh. She turned, gnashing her teeth, chattering in terror, to see a big dog standing near, one paw upraised as he looked at her with savage, yellow eyes. Then, as their eyes met, Queenie's terror died and she uttered a little whine of greeting. It was Lame Leg, her foster-son!

The coyote circled round, sniffing the breeze. He crawled cautiously up to the trap, sniffed it, and backed away with bristling coat, staring at a point just ahead. Clearly he wanted to help her, but this was a peril with which he could not contend. He stood with head raised, waving his tail slowly from side to side; then suddenly he faced up-wind, froze in his tracks, and stood watching, listening, with terrible intentness.

Queenie crouched lower, for she, too, had heard or seen or smelt that dreaded sign. Then down-wind there came, so close that it was like a thunder peal, the awful rumbling growl of a timber wolf! Over the whiteness, full into the starlight he came, walking stiff-legged, very slowly, and with lowered head. His eyes shone like awful balls of fire, saliva dripped from his naked fangs, the huge black mane about his shoulder-blades stood straight on end, adding two inches to his towering stature. It was the black-maned cattle killer on whose scalp lay the bounty – it was Buffalo!

Did the lame little coyote steal away? No, he stood his ground, his legs trembling beneath him, and answered growl for growl. You who know the coyote of the prairies will say: "That was not a coyote trick! More likely he would slink to the nearest ridge and yap!" But I can record only what evidences seem to indicate as facts. Lame Leg held his ground between the big wolf and his helpless foster-mother, and the big wolf paused, wondering at such audacity. Then he charged with an awful chopping of jaws, intent on slashing that coyote to the snow, but the coyote was not there! And behind the very spot where he had stood, within a yard of the trembling Queenie, there rose from the snow a second pair of jaws – rose with a vicious snap, like the snap of wolfish jaws, and the big wolf fell with a roar of terror and dismay.

He rose and shook the snow from his mane. Terrible to behold was he in his impotence, and now he dragged the trap from its setting, hauled the heavy log from its scanty covering, and with a roar turned upon Queenie to avenge his plight.

Snap, slash, snap went the jaws of a coyote, and the big wolf turned, his mask laid open, to face his assailant. Queenie lay trembling and took no part, for between her and the wolf stood her foster-son. The big wolf charged and struck him down, but, hindered by the trap, he could not maintain the advantage of his nimble foe. Snap – slash – snap went the coyote's jaws again, a cloud of powdery snow rose up on the still air, and the fight began.

It was a fight to a finish. For yards all round the snow was trodden flat and smeared and smudged with little stains of brown. "Clank-clank" went the chain of the trap, hurled this way and that; but the dull and slanting jaws kept their hold. There were no witnesses of that awful fight, save the unblinking stars and the cowering, trembling Queenie; but the snow told the story, told of each breathless, ghastly scene in the oldest writing of the world!

When Strychnine Loam came along in the morning he was mystified. There in one of his traps lay the terrier, shivering with cold, strain, and terror. Curled up beside her, apparently still sleeping, was a little coyote with a crippled paw, his coat gashed and rent in a hundred places. He was dead. Farther away, in the centre of that trampled ring, the big black wolf lay stretched in the snow. He, too, was dead. Of the three only the terrier remained alive, and the signs told Wolfer Loam that she was the first to fall to the traps.

A Motherless Cub

◄o►

HUBERT EVANS

Hubert Evans (1892-1986) was born in Vankleek Hill, Ontario, and grew up in Galt, where his father was science teacher at the Galt Collegiate Institute. From childhood excursions to collect nature specimens, camping trips in Muskoka, fishing, muskrat trapping and canoeing in the wilderness, he developed a life-time philosophy: "travel light, have only the essential tools, but keep them sharp and know how to use them." Finding his family's Methodism and Victorian conventionality restrictive, he avoided university by heading west, where he worked on several British Columbia newspapers. In 1915 he enlisted in the Kootenay Battalion and served overseas as a machine gunner. After World War I, Evans found that there was a market for short stories in the United States, where the most saleable kind were "war stories by American guys who'd never been there. I couldn't write about violence," he told his biographer, Alan Twigg, "so I wrote outdoor stories – animal stories." The wilderness areas of British Columbia, where he settled in 1919, provided material for novels, poetry, biography, short fiction and juvenile fiction. Like Charles G.D. Roberts, Evans writes stories that are realistic, unsentimental and clearly focused on a particular incident, but his point of view is less pessimistic. Writing for young people seemed particularly important because "you can still change a person's viewpoint up to the time they're twenty." His most successful series centred on an Airedale named Derry that Evans owned when he lived at Cultis Lake. "A Motherless Cub" is excerpted from Derry . . . of Totem Creek *(1930). Derry's master, Ed, has been hired to protect the wildlife in a lonely area, two hundred miles north of Vancouver, where the most dangerous predators are not animal but human. Other books in the series are* Derry, Airedale of the Frontier *(1928), and* Derry's Partner *(1929). Also of interest is Evans' autobiographical novel* O Time in Your Flight *(1979), which brilliantly recreates his childhood from the perspective of a nine-year-old boy.*

◄o►

E d and Derry were working their way along the sidehill of the valley. Below them a creek ran noisily. Derry scouted ahead. Once when he found bear signs he would have followed the trail hotly, but when Ed examined the tracks, he called him back.

"Likely that's the old lady we bumped into among those vine maples," he decided. "We'll leave her in peace," he added as he struck up the sidehill again to confirm the direction of a line of survey blazes he was following.

Across the creek, on the opposite sidehill, the old bear felt relief at the lessening scent of dog and man. She left off testing the slow air currents and returned to the small cedar where she had been standing when the first alien scent reached her.

Fuzz, her little son, stood shoulder to shoulder with his frolic loving sister. They had been watching their mother, and now both were fascinated by her odd behavior for, during the short time since they had come from the den in the hollow cedar a little way up the slope, she had never done what she was doing this morning.

Fifty feet from them, at the bottom of the slope, the creek foamed and coiled among its scoured boulders. Uncounted rivulets, each carrying snow water from the rugged mountain side, had brought it into noisy freshet. Only at night when the cold from the serene peaks crept lower and glazed the dwindling snow patches with a crust of ice did the creek's jubilant marching chorus become a lullaby.

During the time since their mother had led them from the den, Fuzz and his sister had grown used to the boisterous sound of the stream. A south wind, carrying the crisp sweetness of the spring, stirred the evergreens. For miles and miles along the uneven valley bottom, the tops of cedars, firs and hemlocks were like the spires and minarets of a great city cleansed with sunlight. And in these green lookouts the south wind awoke a myriad little voices whose crooning chorus was a summons for all faithful forest folk to join in the rejoicing because austere winter's siege was at an end. The south wind stirred even the deep thatch of lower branches so that little winking patches of sunlight jigged and swayed upon the forest floor. But these surprising bits of brightness no longer held the attention of the two cubs.

Now they watched their mother with unblinking attention. There was a ludicrous solemnity about the chubby pair as they observed how she reared to her fullest height against the small cedar and then, arching her back, raked the claws of her forefeet through the shredding bark. Those claws, grown uncomfortably long during the months of hibernation, grooved the white sapwood. When the old bear reached up again the heads of both cubs lifted in unison as if they were toys manipulated by an unseen hand. Down came the big pads on the cedar; down, down, came the two muzzles of the cubs, and when she paused at the end of the stroke, the two black buttons which were their noses were pointed unwaveringly at her while expectancy showed in two pairs of little eyes.

The she-bear performed this springtime rite several times more. Then she shook some of the moss and wood dust from her rumpled coat. She yawned, then swung her head slowly, testing the scents of the soft breeze again. The strange scent from man and dog had vanished altogether. On the flats around the creek mouth, miles down the valley, there would be no snow, and green things would be pushing their tender heads through the sodden mat of last year's growth. The dullness of hibernation was leaving her and the urge of hunger was becoming more insistent. Nothing now remained of the deer offal among the vine maples. She shuffled up the slope, led the cubs to the mouth of the den then lay down while they nuzzled and romped about her. There was a positive warmth in the air this morning. She dozed a little, regardless of the cubs who squirmed and tussled between her legs. But soon she got to her feet and, with a soft growl to the cubs which meant, "Follow me," she started purposefully down the slope.

For a time the old bear followed the course of the creek. Its noise handicapped her hearing and exposed her to the hazard of surprise, but she persisted for she knew that creeks sometimes furnished good spring forage and that fish were likely to be stranded on their banks. Lean and hungry after hibernation, and with two cubs to feed, she was eager to reach her spring range. Her pace was necessarily slow but when one of the cubs did not heed her command and fell to cuffing the other lustily, she dealt each a solid spank with the flat of her forepaw. Much subdued, Fuzz and his sister resumed their places close beside her and the journey continued.

From time to time the way led through patches of devil clubs on whose grotesque, spiked stalks buds were already swelling. Sometimes they made detours around windfalls whose tangles the youngsters could not climb. Then unexpectedly the cubs found themselves confronted with a tributary creek. Their mother shuffled upstream a short distance, found a fallen tree which would serve as footlog, and led them onto it.

When he was half way over, Fuzz, awed by the leaping whiteness below him, crouched and gripped the bark with all the strength of his small claws. Then a commanding growl from his mother – and perhaps a recollection of his recent spanking – nerved him to stand up and follow his sister to the far bank.

The way took them farther from the main stream. Its booming sank to a drumming throb coming faintly through the hushed forest. A quarter of a mile farther on, as they were filing past a rotten log, Fuzz saw his mother halt and sniff. Both cubs stood with legs firmly planted and heads low while their mother explored along the moss-covered side of the log. Suddenly she dealt it a resounding blow and lowered her head to listen.

Encouraged by faint sounds of movement from within, she cleared away the moss and began pawing back the earth and fallen needles which, during the course of many seasons, had been banked against the log. Soon she had a hole started. Throwing her weight to her right shoulder and reaching farther and farther under the log, she heaped up crumbling wood and forest mould. At intervals she would pause, push her head into the hole and give a snuffling grunt of inquiry. When she stood back, her face, covered with wood dust, gave her a look of clownish gravity. As she scooped the hole larger, her small eyes were alert for the mice she hoped soon to turn out of their nest.

The first one caught her unprepared. It scampered away under the side of the log. Her forepaw dealt the ground a tremendous blow, then she peered under as she lifted it very carefully. Fuzz and his sister crowded in, filled with the excitement of their first hunting. But when the paw was lifted clear of the ground they looked from the spot up to their mother. There was nothing under the paw and mutely they were inquiring "why?"

Their mother returned brusquely to the hole, her ears forward and a look of pleased eagerness on her discolored face. But no more mice appeared. With a philosophical acceptance of her failure, she grunted to the cubs and started on.

After leaving the log, the old bear led the way to Totem Creek which they must cross here if they were to reach the flats lower down. Soon Fuzz was aware that the booming was growing louder. Ahead, down the aisles between the mottled columns of the cedars, he could see the foaming stream. Seen through the dimness under the big trees, the rushing water showed startlingly white.

For both cubs the creek was an awesome thing. Swollen by a dozen feeders like the one they had crossed, in places it was brimming between its raw cut-banks. Its noise was incessant, more thunderous, in pitch. But when they saw their mother regarding it with indifference, and when she struck off upstream to find the big footlog she had used in other springtimes, they trotted stolidly after her.

A brief search of the bank told the old bear that the footlog had been swept away. She went farther up. From deep in the creek's bed the water-smothered groan and crunch of rolling boulders sounded, and when at the next bend the old bear saw the log jam through which the creek writhed and spouted, she halted and eyed it critically. Then with a grunt to the cubs to trail closely, she went on and found a log on which it was possible to gain the other bank.

Hoisting herself up she tested it with her weight, looking from where its under-scoured stump lay in the wash of the bank to where its top rested on the higher bank opposite. Finding it solid, she growled sharply. Fuzz and his sister scrambled up the roots and stood beside her. Then all three started over.

Fuzz came last. Above his sister's back he could see his mother. Seemingly awkward but sure footed as a cat, she moved slowly on, now and then rallying the timid cubs with grunts of encouragement. Fuzz could feel the chilly, spray laden air current which the lashing surface drew down the creek channel. The sound swelled to a cavernous rumble. But this time his faith in his

mother overcame all fear. So great was his trust that she would take him back to the solid ground that he had not a doubt for his safety. He even looked boldly down at the leaping water.

And then it happened. As he looked down, instinctive caution made him tread slightly off the center of the log on the side opposite to the one past which he was looking. A slab of bark, undermined by insects, came loose with his weight. He clawed vainly and had time for only one frightened squall. Then he went under.

Fuzz never saw his mother bound forward, pause only long enough to make sure the remaining cub would reach the bank, and then charge down the shore in a hopeless attempt to keep abreast of him. Brush crashed, willow thickets swayed as if a tornado was tearing through them as she pounded in pursuit. It was useless. The black head of the cub came up only to be sucked down among the spray drenched logs of the jam. Into the open below he shot, then down the smooth chute at the base of the tangle. Swirls caught him, drew him under, then he was swept to the surface and borne swiftly around the bend.

Had Fuzz been an expert riverman he could not have met the crisis more effectively. Instinct told him it would be fatal to try and fight the hard driving water. It would overwhelm him instantly. Instead he must use it to help him all he could. With body limp and unresisting, he did little more than tread water while he was swept around the bend, into the narrow reach between constricting rock ledges and so into the wider, more broken stretch beyond.

Sometimes his little black head went completely under, but he came up each time, blinded by the water. A quarter of a mile downstream a cross eddy caught him, and he felt his feet touch bottom. The gravel of the sloping bar slipped when he tried to climb out.

He sank back weakly, found firm footing and then, with water streaming from his heaving flanks, he tottered to the dry gravel and sank down in the warming sunlight.

For ten minutes he lay stretched out without once moving. Then when the sun had drawn the chill of the mountain water from his body, he stood up and looked steadily, ruefully, at the stream. He whined petulantly, for he was hungry; then, sitting up on his fat little haunches, he sniffed the air as he had seen his mother do. What scents came to him carried no tidings of a meal. On a tall fir stub overhead the bald headed eagle who fished the ponds below whistled. Fuzz eyed it disapprovingly and then continued his snuffling examination of the gravel.

A short time later, while his mother still searched the far bank above the bend, Fuzz, tiring of the bar, sat back, carefully licked the crescent of white fur on his chest and then, as if that had prepared him for all emergencies, he ambled off downstream.

Like all wild animals, Fuzz saved himself from a great deal that day by being incapable of the human error of feeling sorry for himself. Like even the adult furred and feathered folk, when left in their natural state, he was made immune from worry by that child-like faith which knowing Man terms "brute ignorance" but which even to the animals can be the most sure and fortifying wisdom.

Evening found him more hungry than ever. Once, long after dark, he was circling a clump of small alders when a deer bounded up, its sharp front hoofs stabbing the moss in timid defiance. Fuzz sat up, his forepaws dangling; then the deer snorted and vanished in one clean, swinging jump.

Soon after, Fuzz found shelter beneath a windfall and stayed there until the searching fingers of the dawn began unravelling the thick tapestry of night. Then he got up, passed beyond the windfall and trudged down the valley. An hour later he heard a strange excited sound. And the sound was bearing swiftly down on him!

Fuzz sat up, waiting. He had never heard the bark of a dog before. The sound ceased and he was about to go on when the soft staccato of speeding paws came from behind him. He whirled in time to see a black and tan animal rush from the brush and make straight for him.

Suddenly aware that he had overtaken the cub, Derry swerved adroitly. The flashing swipe which Fuzz aimed at him did not alarm the Airedale, for he had learned to dodge such blows from full grown bears. Derry began to circle, barking for Ed to come, and at the same time preventing the cub from galloping away into the woods by darting in every time Fuzz turned to run. A moment later Ed, who had been quietly patrolling the sidehill below the end of the hidden trail to Beaver Cove, came upon the scene.

The appearance of this second creature alarmed Fuzz still more, but he stood his ground manfully, sitting back with paws dangling, ready to deal blows to left and right.

"Watch him, son," Ed commanded. Then with the utmost caution he began searching the surrounding thickets for signs of the she-bear. The cub began to squall so lustily for help that Ed, who was unarmed, was ready to make a quiet withdrawal if he so much as found a track of the she-bear. At such times mother bruin was likely to charge first and investigate the visitor's intentions later.

But a skillful examination of the ground revealed the fact that the cub had wandered here unescorted. This surprised Ed. She-bears were among the most zealous mothers in the woods and to come upon an unescorted cub meant that disaster had overtaken the little family. An ugly suspicion entered his mind. He would come back here to try and learn the truth. But in the meantime something had to be done with the unprotected cub. Ed began peeling off his mackinaw jumper.

"Razz him a bit," he instructed the terrier and then, holding the coat in front of him, he advanced upon Fuzz. A moment later, the writhing and squealing cub had been muffled in the coat and was being carried quickly away.

Fuzz was still resisting when the coat was unwrapped and he kicked loose only to find himself in Ed's new cabin and with the closed door blocking his escape.

"Easy, big boy, easy," Ed advised as Fuzz, now in the far corner, assumed a pose which would have done credit to a heavyweight boxer. Outside Derry clawed vainly at the door asking to be let in to share the fun.

"He'll give you all the fun you're looking for in a day or so," Ed promised as he closed the door behind him and crossed to the site of his former camp. Among a few other unneeded things he had left there was an empty vinegar bottle, which Ed partly filled with water at the spring before going back to the cabin. Once inside he put some milk powder and sugar into it. After shaking it he took a piece of rag from his pack, wrapped it around the bottle neck and came toward the sulking prisoner.

Fuzz fought him, only to be overpowered and have his jaws forced open. Something wet and soft was pushed into his mouth. He wriggled to get free of it and then, having been made to taste it, his hostility vanished. He closed his black lips around the bottle neck and with head up began sucking down the sweetened milk.

Ed stood back, grinning, while Fuzz tilted it rakishly with both paws and drained it with a rapt singleness of purpose which showed Ed he had been many hours without his mother.

From that very morning Fuzz accepted his new surroundings in as matter-of-fact a way as he had the accident which separated him from his mother. He made himself thoroughly at home and with an infectious drollery he soon was inviting Derry to romp with him.

Derry needed no second invitation. For hours at a time he and Fuzz would indulge in mock battles and when the game became too realistic Fuzz would take "time out" by simply climbing the nearest tree from whose lower branches he would glare impishly at the playmate he had outwitted.

When Ed was in camp, Fuzz would follow him about, always on the watch for food. It was this appetite of his which brought him rebukes from Derry every time he became too interested in the food cached inside the cabin. Derry's sudden change to sternness and his warning growls let the cub see that these things must not be tampered with.

During the daytime, when Ed and Derry were away, Fuzz made no effort to leave the little clearing. He wandered contentedly near the cabin, sometimes interested in everything from brush piles to butterflies, sometimes drowsing in the sun.

"You're a wise little duffer," Ed told him one night. "If only you could talk I bet there'd be somebody over Beaver Cove way would want to stop your mouth. What was the use of shooting your mother anyhow?" Ed thought hotly.

The thought that the she-bear had been killed by a poacher made Ed bitter against the Beaver Cove people. Killing deer he could understand, but to slay a she-bear, soon after she left her den with two helpless cubs, was stupid destruction. Her hide would be useless until she had been active for some weeks, and she would be unfit for food. Like most people who live close to nature, wanton destruction of wild life filled Ed with resentment. To kill for food was one thing, but to kill for the sake of killing was both senseless and criminal.

The Dark-eyed Doe

◄○►

KERRY WOOD

Kerry Wood (b. 1907) was born in New York of Scottish parents. In 1918 his family settled in Red Deer, Alberta, where Wood has lived ever since. During the past seventy years he has produced twenty-three books, six thousand short stories and eight thousand articles. For many years his was a familiar voice on Edmonton's CKUA radio, broadcasting nature talks and childhood reminiscences. Among his many honours are an honorary doctorate, two Governor-General's awards for juvenile fiction and a Vicky Metcalfe Award "for consistently good writing of material inspirational to Canadian youth." He rather regrets having "turned down an Indian chieftain-ship at a time when it mattered." Wood belongs to the tradition of artist-naturalist which Ernest Thompson Seton established. "The

Dark-eyed Doe," set in a characteristic Alberta landscape, exemplifies an animal's ability to base its response to habitat on learned experience. Wood's publications include Willowdale *(1956), from which this story comes,* Three Mile Bend *(1945),* Wild Winter *(1954),* Mickey the Beaver and Other Stories *(1964) and such historical works as* The Queen's Cowboy: Colonel Macleod of the Mounties *(1960) and* The Great Chief: Maskepetoon, Warrior of the Crees *(1957). The well-known Canadian artist Illingworth Kerr contributed pen-and-ink drawings as headpieces for* Willowdale's *fifteen stories. The collection is dedicated to "a lovely wife who laughs and sometimes cries as she proof-reads my stories."*

There is a wild ravine on the far side of Blackbird Lake, north-east of the town limits. To reach the ravine, one has to penetrate some dense underbrush and go beyond the creeklet which trickles down the draw. Alders and willows crowd each other on the stream banks on the flats near the lake, while thickets of saskatoon and chokecherries thrive on the slopes above. Then the shrubs give way to forest growth, where spruces reach high to get their share of sunshine. White birches and smooth-barked poplars are scattered among the evergreens. In fact, the whole ravine area looks like an untidy but very beautiful park. It was there that the blind deer had her home.

A few deer have always lived in the woodlands near the pond, as it is the last large wooded area close to Willowdale. The wasteland totals more than two hundred acres of forested slopes and valleys, centred by the pond with its summer coating of yellow water-lilies. Jonathan Gates has farm fields on the uplands nearby, but he always saved the trees around Blackbird Lake. The deadfalls provide him with a perpetual supply of firewood, while he likes the idea of preserving the wilderness as a small sanctuary for game and birds. He was delighted that a few deer stayed there, and to one doe a blind fawn was born.

How the little creature survived is a mystery. Coyotes howl every night from the hills above the pond; some say that these wild dogs are not above seeking out the hidden bed of a weak fawn. Once a black bear was sighted among the berry bushes next the Lake, while Mr. Gates himself has heard the yowling scream of a Canada Lynx from the woodlands. Yet despite all these wild hunters, the blind fawn grew to adult size and was finally deserted by its mother. Then the sightless deer chose a range in the park-like ravine.

Willowdale's game warden, Don Cully, was the first to discover her affliction. Don roused the doe from a thicket one day. She turned directly towards him for a couple of jumps before going carefully around a massive tree and heading into the screening alders.

"She didn't scoot straight away like you'd expect, and that made me wonder. Mind, I had no idea right then that she was blind. At the time it just seemed to me that she was following a trail I couldn't see."

The next time Cully glimpsed her, she had her ears flagged towards him and was half hidden behind some saskatoons. Don stalked fairly close, then used binoculars to get a better look at her and the magnification gave him a chance to see the film covering her eyes. When he went closer still she became uneasy and moved. Don saw how cautiously she turned, feeling her way through the shrubbery before bounding down the slope in a zig-zag course that missed all trees, deadfalls, and other obstructions.

"I'm positive that she's got a system of trails all through her home territory. Maybe her sense of smell helps her to identify those paths, but my own guess is that she's memorized the routes by the feel of ground contours or the touch of twigs at certain places which guide her along the proper trail. It was marvellous to watch her, totally blind and yet going so swiftly down that slope to reach the thickets near the creek."

Once in the willows she moved like a shadow and was soon beyond the warden's view. He made a habit of visiting Blackbird Lake and its surroundings quite often from then on, just for the pleasure of watching her.

"I tell you, fellows; there's something real special about her. She has more grace than any ordinary deer, because there's a poise about her that is lovely to see."

Cully didn't tell many about her, of course. Don is no fool, and he is always close-mouthed when hunters try to get information from him about the best deer ranges in our Willowdale outlands. The warden is not mean about such matters, but it is his job to protect and conserve the diminishing game of our district. Hence Don Cully told only a few good friends about that blind doe. He mentioned her to Jonathan Gates, the land-owner, also to Tom David, the policeman. Once the warden guided in the Reverend Tanner to show him the deer, because Cully knew that the minister would sense the proud independence of that blind animal and would fully appreciate the pathetic yet beautiful quality of her affliction. The warden also took in Maryellen Haskell, who painted a fine picture of the deer posed among the shining birches.

Naturally, Don made no mention of the doe to men like Warty Sloane. There are trashy people in every community, and the warden knew well enough that Sloane bragged of his fondness for venison poached out of season.

Yet it was impossible to hush all talk of such an oddity. Before long most of the townsfolk and nearby farmers had heard about the blind beauty of Blackbird Lake. A few went blundering in there to get a look, but she was much too secretive for most of them. Young Morton, the minister's boy, tried to stalk the doe by woodcraft methods he'd learned at boy scout meetings. He didn't see her after more than an hour's searching, so Morton gave up the quest. Then, boy-like, he pushed over a large stump that had an ant-riddled and rotten base. The crash of this tree falling to earth was terrifically loud, and the noise startled the deer from her hiding-place. Morton described how she came bounding up the slope towards him and carefully following one of her invisible pathways. That stump had fallen directly across her trail, and she smashed into it and fell. For a moment she was completely still with shock, then she struggled onto her feet again and stood trembling, undecided about what to do. Next the doe slowly felt her way all around the stump until she reached the familiar path once more, then went swiftly on into the spruces and out of sight.

"That ole stump was sure heavy," Morton related. "It was all I could do to move it, but I used a pry and I finally shifted it alongside another fallen log. I left it there, so's it would be out of the blind deer's way when she came along there again."

Don Cully told us that the doe did not forget the tumble. From then on she made a careful half-circle around the vacant place where the stump had been lying when she hit it.

"I don't mind admitting that it brought a lump into my throat, seeing her do that and thinking of the slow and painful way she must have learned each of her trails through that ravine."

The warden described how she fed on birch browse and willow twigs; how she went to a favourite meadow and knelt, deer-fashion, to graze on clover leaves. She had a special path to a drinking-pool, a spring-fed cup at the edge of the creeklet. Her morning bed was usually up in the high part of the ravine on a knoll screened by chokecherry bushes. At evening she liked to forage in the lowlands next the lake and bed down among the alders in one of the thickest tangles of the region.

"Coyotes won't bother her at all, now that she's full-grown," Don said. "Besides, coyotes have lots of mice and rabbits to feed on these days. Larger predators like cougar and wolves seldom venture this close to town, so I believe she'll be safe from all harm."

She thrived there on the far side of Blackbird Lake until autumn came. That's the time when stately bucks go questing for consorts, and Don Cully found larger tracks along the creek to indicate that the blind doe had a mate. The game warden patrolled the area a great deal after the first snowfall, when deer hunters were abroad in numbers. But all the sportsmen, like Frew and Pete Popovitch and others, by some unspoken agreement among themselves stayed away from the Jonathan Gates lands to avoid frightening that beautiful, sightless animal.

When winter ended and Hermit Thrushes had returned to the ravine, the doe had her fawn in a hidden part of the willow thickets. Cully reported that he'd never seen such a devoted mother. She taught her little one all the special secrets of caution, all the wary tricks of testing the breeze for scent of enemies and listening for warnings of danger: the chirring scold of a squirrel, the three-note call of crows, the shrill alarms of bluejays and kakking of magpies, and the meaningful slap of a beaver's tail on the quiet waters of the lake.

"It's a young stag," Don told us. "He's a little beauty, too. I saw them at the spring pool this morning, and the wee one was nursing while the mother stood patient and proud. I wish Maryellen could have seen it and painted us a picture of that scene."

As summer advanced the young fawn was no longer left in a hidden retreat, but began following the blind mother through the woodlands on her feeding jaunts. A few berry-pickers sighted the doe and her sturdy youngster; in fact, the animals were nibbling on purple-ripe saskatoons at the time. Miss Hagen's class of Grade Five students, out on a September flower-gathering expedition during the first week of school, came excitedly back to town to tell of getting a good close look at the beautiful doe and her half-grown fawn.

Yes; by this time everyone around Willowdale knew about that blind deer at Blackbird Lake. Warty Sloane had heard of her, and had slipped furtively out there a few times when he knew the game warden was busy elsewhere. Sloane had a sly craft that his illegal activities made necessary, hence it was easy for him to stalk the doe and learn something about her habits and routine. He thought up a plan to get her, though he waited until frosts became sharp to put

the venison in prime condition. Then Sloane went out to Blackbird Lake early one morning. Once at the ravine, he looped some cabled wire down from a tough birch branch under which the doe passed on her way to the spring pool. The poacher had chosen a snare in preference to a rifle, because he knew that shot noise might bring the warden on the run.

But by chance Don Cully was in that ravine, at the very moment when Sloane was reaching a knife towards the throat of the poor blind doe who was frantically jerking against the relentless noose. The game warden charged across the clearing, yelling at Sloane to drop the knife. Warty Sloane did drop it, too, and sprinted away before Cully could reach him. Don didn't bother to chase the poacher. Instead, he snatched up the heavy knife and quickly sliced through the copper wire to release the gasping doe.

She whirled away with her frightened fawn at her side. The death-struggle had numbed the doe's instincts and the deer didn't follow one of her familiar trails at that moment. She bounded heedlessly over the rough growth, grazing past one large tree and crashing headlong through a grove of sapling poplars. Beyond the poplars the fawn dug in its tiny hooves and skidded to a stop as he bleated a wild alarm. Instantly the doe whirled and went to her little one.

Her quick devotion saved her life. One more bound, and she would have gone over a sheer cliff to crash on the jagged creek rocks below. But now, nuzzling her fawn she stood quiet until the panic of the murderous episode had passed.

"She's not hurt," Cully assured us. "I watched her feel her way back to a trail, then they went loping off together into the chokecherries to seek a day-bed. We haven't lost our blind beauty, and from now on everyone of you can help guard her."

As for Warty Sloane, he moved out of Willowdale after he paid the heavy fine that Judge Benn imposed on him. At that trial Sloane must have finally sensed that there are forms of blindness that decent folk just won't tolerate.

Master Rabbit and
the Bad Wild Cat

◄○►

PETER LUM

Peter Lum (1911-1983) was the nom-de-plume *of Lady Crowe. Widely travelled, she developed an expertise in East Asian studies and an eclectic interest in myths and folktales. The following selection was published in* Folk Tales from North America *(1973). Other works are* Fabulous Beasts *(1952) and* The Stars in Our Heaven: Myths and Fables *(1948).*

A vivid character in native Canadian mythology and folklore is the trickster. Of great antiquity, he may be greedy, impudent, obscene, dishonest and treacherous or helpful, good-humoured, witty and benevolent. According to Paul Radin in The Trickster: A Study in American Indian Mythology *(1956), he combined in one figure the polarities of life-creation and destruction, altruism and* self-indulgence, intelligence and stupidity. Like many supernatural characters who appear in our native peoples' literature and art, he has both animal and human forms but, unlike European shape-shifters, the animal form is dominant. He might be Raven, Crow or Coyote. The Eastern Woodlands Indians call him Rabbit.

Ordinarily, a lynx hunting a rabbit in the eastern forests would likely be successful. In Wild Captives, W.G. Dodds gives a realistic account of a normal event:

> The rabbit was staying close now to the form or lair she used during most of the daylight hours. She would venture only a few yards for green food, fresh twig growth, or cool water from the little brook. A few more yards down the path, she would turn to face her resting-place and feed slowly back. . . . Suddenly she tensed. There was something else! Without hearing, or smelling it, she sensed something else. Then she gave a short 'click,' hopped about to face the opposite direction, and screamed as she was at once covered with a dark weight and held by claws that pierced her flesh, heart, and lungs.

But Master Rabbit, like Brer Rabbit in Joel Chandler's folktales, uses imagination, knowledge of psychology, disguise, lies, tempta-tion – and a little magic – to outwit and humiliate his enemy. Representations of Rabbit can be seen in the art of Ojibwa artist Norval Morrisseau.

◄o►

When Rabbit was very young he used to try and imitate other animals, and he was always getting things wrong. Finally he realized that if he used his own imagination, and did things in his own way, he could outwit most of the other animals, even those who were much bigger and stronger than he was. It took years of practice. Then he became Master Rabbit, a great Magician.

He still had plenty of enemies. The most dangerous of these was Bad Wild Cat, a lynx, very quick, very treacherous, and very persistent. He was determined to track down Master Rabbit, and so he set out across the snow one fine winter's morning in search of his prey. Winter was the best time for hunting because then all rabbit tracks showed up clearly; and Bad Wild Cat had a very good idea where to start looking for the Rabbit.

Master Rabbit knew instinctively that the Wild Cat was on his trail. He picked up a handful of magic chips, thin and flat, which left no mark on the snow. He threw the first one as far as he could, took a great leap, and landed on it. He threw the second as far as he could, and leapt on to that. He went on like this until he had used up all the chips except one, and then he set off on his own feet, as fast as he could. He ran all day, until the setting sun cast long, blue shadows from each tree across the white snow. Then he stopped, trampled down a small circle of snow, stuck a branch from a nearby tree upright in the middle of this circle, and sat down to wait.

Wild Cat meanwhile had found the Rabbit gone, with smooth snow on every side of his hut; not a rabbit's print was to be seen anywhere. Wild Cat however was no fool when it came to following a trail. He ran quickly around and around the hut, making a wider circle each time, but each time making sure he came full circle; that way, it was only a matter of time before he caught up with the tracks. Then he set off at full speed, faster than any rabbit could run.

The trail led him to a fine-looking wigwam standing all alone in the midst of the snow-covered woods. When he stuck his head inside the wigwam he saw a nice-looking old man, with grey hair, smoking a pipe. He had rather long ears, but old men often do have long ears, so Bad Wild Cat thought little of that.

"Have you seen a rabbit running this way?" he asked.

"Rabbit?" said the old man. "Why, we have hundreds of rabbits around here. You can see one every day."

"Well, yes, perhaps. But I was following the trail of one particular rabbit, and it led me here."

"He probably ran around the edge of my wigwam and into the woods," the old man told him. "If I were you, I wouldn't bother about it tonight. You must be tired and hungry. Why not have some supper and stay the night here?"

The fire was so warm, and supper smelled so good, that Wild Cat readily agreed. He went to sleep feeling warm and well-fed, dreaming of how he would catch up with Master Rabbit next day. Alas for him! He woke up at sunrise lying in the open, in the snow, wet, cold, hungry, and absolutely furious at having been tricked.

He followed Master Rabbit's trail again all that day. But this time Rabbit had had more time to make ready. He trampled down a whole field of snow, scattered branches everywhere, and whispered a few very effective spells which sounded rather like the multiplication table. By the time Bad Wild Cat had followed his trail over a hill and down to this snowfield there was a whole Indian village. People were walking around, fetching water from the well, lighting their fires, and preparing the evening meal.

Wild Cat stopped the first man he saw, a nice-looking young man, even if his ears did stand up rather like the ears of a pitcher.

"Have you seen a rabbit running this way?" he asked.

"Rabbits? Rabbits? Why, the place is infested with rabbits. I certainly would not go looking for one."

"This is a particular rabbit I am looking for. Master Rabbit, they call him."

"I wouldn't know anything about that," the young man told him. "Why not come along to the Village Chief with me? He knows everything."

So they went along to the largest, best-built wigwam in the village, where Bad Wild Cat was welcomed by the Village Chief and his two beautiful daughters. The Chief was a fine looking man, with grey hair so thick that long tufts stood up on either side of his head, almost like ears. He knew nothing more about rabbits than the young man did, but he insisted that Wild Cat stay the night with him and his daughters. They had a delicious meal and then Wild Cat went to sleep on a soft, fleecy White Bear's skin, the smell of the cedar-wood bark from which the wigwam was built fragrant all around him, and the firelight dancing before him.

He woke up in a cedar swamp, lying on wet snow, with a bad cut in his head where he must have fallen on a stone, thinking that it was a pillow. He was starving, for of course magic food has no nourishment whatsoever.

This time Wild Cat swore that he would not be taken in again. But by the time evening came, and he had been following Master Rabbit's trail all day, his head was throbbing with pain, and he badly needed a doctor to look at the wound. He stopped at the first of two wigwams, where a kindly old man, wearing a long feather on either side of his head, immediately sent his daughter into the village to fetch a doctor. When the doctor came, he too was a kindly old man, with grey hair, parted in the centre so that it was almost like two horns sticking out over his ears. Tired and suffering as he was, it did seem to Wild Cat that he looked rather like a rabbit. It wasn't only the hair; he had a split nose, and the soles of his feet were yellow.

"Before you look at my head," he said to the doctor, "would you mind telling me why your nose is split like that of a rabbit?"

"A very sad story," the doctor told him. "I was cutting some shells to make into wampum beads when the stone on which I was carving them split in two, and one of the flying pieces of stone was so sharp that it slit my nose right through, just as you see. It was very painful at the time, I can tell you."

"It must have been," Wild Cat agreed. "And how does it happen that the soles of your feet are yellow, like a rabbit's?"

"Why that is quite common, if you are a smoker. When I am fixing the tobacco for my pipe I need both hands to work it with, so I always hold it steady with my feet. You know how tobacco stains."

With this, Bad Wild Cat was satisfied. He let the doctor put some cooling ointment on his wound, while the daughter of the kindly old man who owned the wigwam cooked his supper and put him to bed. She even left a pitcher of wine beside him, saying that a good drink would help him get to sleep.

He slept. But he woke up again in a snowy field, starving, cold and wet. The wound in his head was stuffed full of pine needles, which of course made it worse. Beside him on the ground was an old pitcher-plant, filled with dirty water.

By this time however Master Rabbit was running out of magic, and it was a great strain putting on a new performance every night. On the following day he was only just ahead of Bad Wild Cat when he came to a great lake, much too wide and deep to cross. But he still had one trick left, the best of all. He had a single chip of wood, larger than those he had used to keep from leaving footprints around his hut, and not so flat. Now he twirled this around his head, threw it as far out into the lake as he could, and jumped aboard. It had become a ship, a ship much bigger than even the biggest canoe any Indian would use. It was more like the ships that the white men sailed in when they came to North America, and it had three big guns on either side. Master Rabbit appeared as the captain of the ship, wearing a beautiful cocked hat, crossways, the two points sticking out on either side of his head just like ears.

Bad Wild Cat was not fooled by this. "No more of your magic!" he cried. "This time I recognize you, and this time I am going to get even with you."

He started to swim out to the ship. If he once got on board, that would certainly be the end of the ship and of Master Rabbit as well. But he had reckoned without the guns. Master Rabbit summoned up his last ounce of magic, and off went the guns with such a roar that Wild Cat was scared almost out of his wits. Maybe the ship was only magic, he thought, maybe Master Rabbit's beautiful cocked hat was only to cover his long ears, but those guns sounded real. He turned tail, swam back to shore as fast as he possibly could, and fled into the shelter of the woods, so frightened that as far as anyone knows he may still be running.

Big Small and
Little Small

◄○►

ARCHIBALD STANSFELD BELANEY
(GREY OWL)

Archibald Stansfeld Belaney (1888-1938) was the real name of an author better known as Grey Owl. His friend and publisher, Lovat Dickson, in a 1973 biography called him "Wilderness Man" and Anahareo, his Iroquois wife (one of several) "Devil in Deerskins." In 1933, when Belaney sent Dickson his first manuscript, he claimed mixed blood – son of a Scots father and an Apache mother. A mingling of truth and fantasy characterized many of his relationships. In fact, he was an Englishman who had been brought up in Hastings by two maiden aunts. He had emigrated to Canada at fifteen, returned to fight as a sniper in World War I and then settled permanently in Canada in 1917. In 1930, "Grey Owl" or "Wa-Sha-Quon-Asin" ("He-Who-Walks-By-Night") displaced "Archie

Belaney." Thenceforth, he assumed the trappings of a Métis – deer-skin clothing, moccasins, canoe, dark hair worn in braids.

Not least among the contradictions inherent in this enigmatic personality was the fact that, having supported himself by trapping beaver and contributing to the virtual extinction of the species in some areas of Ontario and Quebec, he became their "brother," a dedicated conservationist. The turning point had come in 1928 when Anahareo and Grey Owl had taken into their camp two beaver kittens whose mother had died in a trap. The kittens were named McGinty and McGinnis, and their exploits provided the material for Pilgrims of the Wild *(1934). In the following year appeared* The Adventures of Sajo and Her Beaver People, *from which the following story is taken.*

◄O►

The kittens quickly took a liking to their new way of living, and although no human beings could ever quite take the place of their own parents, everything possible was done to make them feel at ease.

Shapian partitioned off the under part of his bunk with sheets of birch bark, leaving one end open; and this was their house, in which they at once made themselves very much at home. Gitchie Meegwon cut a hole in the floor and fitted down into it a wash-tub, for a pond – not much of a one, perhaps, but it was as large as the plunge-hole had been, and they spent nearly half their time in it, and would lie on top of the water eating their twigs and leaves.

Whenever they left the tub, they always squatted their plump little persons upright beside it, and scrubbed their coats, first squeezing the hair in bunches with their little fists to get the water out. That done, the whole coat was carefully combed with a double claw that all beavers are provided with, one on each hind foot, for this purpose. All this took quite a while, and they were so business-like and serious about it that Sajo would become as interested as they were, and would sometimes help them, rubbing their fur this way and that with the tips of her fingers, and then they would scrub away so much the harder.

It was their fashion, when drying themselves off in this way, to raise one arm high up above their heads, as far as it would go, and rub that side with the other hand, and being upright as they were, it looked as if they were about to dance the Highland Fling. They often sat up in this manner while eating the bark off small sticks, and as one or other of them held a stick crossways in his hands, rolling it round and round whilst the busy teeth whittled off the bark, he looked for all the world like some little old man playing on a flute. Sometimes they varied the show, and when the sticks were very slim they ate the whole business, putting one end in their mouths and pushing it in with their hands, while the sharp front teeth, working very fast, chopped it into tiny pieces. The rattle of their cutting machinery sounded much the same as would a couple of sewing-machines running a little wild, and as they held up their heads and shoved the sticks, to all appearances, slowly down their throats, they looked a good deal like a pair of sword-swallowers who found a meal of swords very much to their taste.

They had to have milk for the first two weeks or so, and Sajo borrowed a bottle and a baby's nipple from a neighbour in the village, and fed them with it turn about. But while one would be getting his meal (both hands squeezed tight around the neck of the bottle!), the other would scramble around and make a loud outcry and a hubbub, and try to get hold of the bottle, and there would be a squabbling and a great confusion, and the can of milk was sometimes upset and spilled all over; so that at last there had to be another bottle and nipple found, and Shapian fed one while Sajo fed the other. Later on they were fed bannock and milk, which made things a little easier, as each had his own small dish which the children held for him. The beavers would pick up the mixture with one hand, shoving it into their mouths at a great rate; and I am afraid their table manners were not very nice, as there was a good deal of rather loud smacking of lips and hard breathing to be heard, and they often talked with their mouths full. But they had one excellent point, which not all of us have, and liked to put away their dishes when they had finished, pushing them along the floor into a corner or under the stove; of course if there was a certain amount of milk-soaked bannock left in them, that was quite all right, so far as the beavers were concerned, and by the time the dishes had arrived at their destinations these remains had been well squashed and trampled on the line of march, and the floor would be nicely marked up with small, sticky beaver tracks, having sometimes to be partly scrubbed; and Sajo always collected the little dishes and washed them up, the same as she did those of the "big people." Being fed separately, each of them came to look on one of the children as his special friend, and one of them would go to each when they were called. At first they had no names, and the children just called

"Undaas, undaas, Amik, Amik,"* which means "Come here, come here, Beaver, Beaver." But a little later on Sajo remembered the day that the two wooden dolls had seemed to be looking on when the kittens first had come, and how these new arrivals had so quickly taken their place; well, she thought, they may as well take their names as well, and so she called the beavers Chilawee and Chikanee,† which means Big Small and Little Small. And the larger one of the two was called Chilawee, or Big Small, and the not-so-large one was called Chikanee, or Little Small. And so they both got their names; and the names suited them very well too, because, after all, they *were* very small and they *did* look a lot like a pair of woolly toys that had come to life and stepped down off a shelf. And it was not long before they got to know these names, and would always come out from the house under Shapian's bunk when called on; but the names sounded so much alike, that when one was called they both would come, and as they themselves were as much alike as two peas, the difference in size being not very great, it was often pretty hard to tell which was which. And to make matters worse, they did not grow evenly; that is, one would grow a little faster than the other for a while, and then he would slack down and the other would catch up, and get ahead of him. First one was bigger than the other, then the other was bigger than the one! And it would be discovered that Little Small had been Big Small for quite some time, whilst Big Small had been going around disguised as Little Small. No sooner would that be fixed up than they would

---

* Pronounced Am-*mick*.
† Pronounced *Chill*-a-wee and Chik-a-*nee*.

change sizes again, and when they evened up, in the middle stages as it were, they could not by any means be told apart.

It was all very confusing, and Sajo had just about decided to give them one name between them and call them just "The Smalls," when Chilawee settled matters after a manner all his own. He had a habit of falling asleep in the warm cave under the stove, between the stones, and one day there was a great smell of burning hair, and no one could imagine where it came from. The stove was opened and examined, and swept off, and the stove-pipes were tapped, and rapped, but the smell of burning hair was getting stronger all the time; until someone thought of looking *under* the stove, to discover Chilawee sleeping there unconcernedly while the hair on his back scorched to a crisp, and he was routed out of there with a large patch of his coat badly singed. This made a very good brand, something like those that cattle are marked with on a ranch, and it stayed there all Summer, making it very easy to tell who was who; and by calling one of them (the burnt one) *Chil*awee, and the other Chika*nee*, so as to be a little different, they got to know each their name, and everything was straightened out at last.

They were a great pair of little talkers, Chilawee and Chikanee, and were always jabbering together, and sometimes made the strangest sounds. And whenever either of the children spoke to them, which was often, they nearly always answered in a chorus of little bleats and squeals. When there was any work going on, such as the carrying in of water, or wood, or the floor was being swept, or if the people laughed and talked more than usual, or there were any visitors, the two of them would come bouncing out to see what it was all about and try to join in, and they would cut all kinds of capers, and get pretty generally in the way. It had been found that if given any titbits from the table, they always took them into their house to eat or store them. So when they, like bad children, got to be something of a nuisance to the visitors, they had to be bribed with bits of bannock to make them go back in again; but before long, out they would come for some more bannock, and take that in with them, and out again, and so on. And very soon they got to know that visiting time was bannock time as well, and when meal-times came around they knew all about that too, and would be right there, pulling and tugging at the people's clothes and crying out for bannock, and trying to climb up people's legs to get it. And of course they always got what they wanted, and would run off with it to their cabin under the bunk, shaking their heads and hopping along in great style.

They followed the children around continuously, trotting patiently along behind them; and their legs were so very short and they ran so low to the floor on them, that their feet could hardly be seen, so that they looked like two little clockwork animals out of a toy-shop, that went on wheels and had been wound up and never *would* stop. Anything they found on the floor, such as moccasins, kindling wood and so forth, they dragged from place to place, and later, when they got bigger and stronger, they even stole sticks of firewood from the woodbox and took them away to their private chamber, where they sliced them up into shavings with their keen-edged teeth and made their beds with them; and nice, clean-looking beds they were too. Any small articles of cloth-ing that might happen to fall to the floor, if not picked up at once, quickly disappeared into the beaver house. The broom would be pulled down and hauled around, and this broom and the fire-wood seemed to be their favourite playthings; chiefly, I suspect, on

account of the noise they could make with them, which they seemed very much to enjoy.

But their greatest amusement was wrestling. Standing up on their hind legs, they would put their short arms around each other as far as they would go, and with their heads on each others' shoulders, they would try to put each other down. Now, this was hard to do, as the wide tails and the big, webbed hind feet made a very solid support, and they would strain, and push, and grunt, and blow until one of them, feeling himself slipping, would begin to go backwards in order to keep his balance, with the other coming along pushing all he could. Sometimes the loser would recover sufficiently to begin pushing the other way, and then the walk would commence to go in the opposite direction; and so, back and forth, round and round, for minutes at a time, they would carry on this strange game of theirs, which looked as much like two people waltzing as it did anything else. All the while it was going on there would be, between the grunts and gasps, loud squeals and cries from whoever was getting pushed, and much stamping of feet and flopping of tails, trying to hold their owners up, until one of them, on the backward march, would allow his tail to double under him, and fall on his back, when they would immediately quit and scamper around like two madcaps. It was all done in the greatest good humour, and the two children never grew tired of watching them.

And between this uproarious exhibition, and the flute-playing, and the sword-swallowing, and the begging, the trundling around of wood and all the other racket and commotion that, on some days, only ceased when they went to sleep, they were about as busy, and noisy, and amusing a pair of little people as you could wish to live with.

But they were not always so lively. There came times when they were very quiet, when they would sit solemnly down together with their hands held tight to their chests and their tails before them, watching whatever was going on, still as two mice, looking, listening without a word, as though they were trying to make out what everything was all about. And sometimes, as they squatted there one beside the other, like two chocolate-coloured kewpies or little mannikins, Sajo would kneel in front of them and tell them a story, marking time to the words with her finger before their noses, as though she were conducting an orchestra. And they would sit there and listen, and watch her finger very closely, and soon they would commence to shake their heads up and down and from side to side, as beaver always do when they are pleased, and at last they would shake their whole bodies and their heads so hard that they would topple over and roll on the floor, exactly as if they had understood every word and just couldn't help laughing themselves to pieces over the story.* And Shapian would stand by taking it all in, and finding it rather ridiculous; but at the same time he wished – very privately of course – that he was not quite such a man, so he could join in this storytelling business himself. There were times when this thing of being grown up rather interfered with the fun!

Sometimes the little fellows were lonely, and would whimper together with small voices in their dark little chamber, and Sajo, who had never forgotten her own mother and knew why they were

---

* This is actual fact, as are all the animal actions described in the story. Young beavers, raised by hand, will often respond in this manner to the advances of a person they know well. Wild beaver communicate their emotions to one another in this and other very striking ways.

lonesome, would take them in her arms and croon softly to them, and try to comfort them. And they would snuggle up close to her, holding tight to each other's fur all the while as though afraid to lose one another, and would bury their wee noses in the warm, soft spot in her neck where they so loved to be; and after a while the whimpering would cease and they would perhaps forget, for this time, and they would give big, long sighs and little moans of happiness, and fall asleep.

For, after all, with all their mischief and their shouting and their fun, they were just two small lost waifs, and they gave to these two human children, in their own humble way, the same love they had given to the father and the mother they had lost, and whom they never would forget.

And especially Chikanee loved Sajo. Chikanee was not as strong as Chilawee, was quieter and more gentle. Chilawee had a rather jolly way about him, and was more of a roisterer, one of those "all for fun and fun for all" kind of lads to whom life is just one big joke; but Chikanee often had lonesome spells by himself, in corners, and had to be picked up, and petted, and made much of. Often he came out in the night and cried beside Sajo's bed to be taken up and allowed to sleep there beside her – while Chilawee lay on his back in the hut, snoring away like a good fellow. When Chikanee was in some small trouble, such as bumping his nose on the stove, or getting the worst of a wrestling match, he came to Sajo for comfort. And Sajo, always ready to sympathise with him because he was the weaker of the two, would kneel down beside him on the floor; and then Chikanee would climb onto her lap and lie there, happy and contented. Chilawee, when his badness was all done for the day, and he was feeling perhaps a little left out of things, would come over to get *his* share of the petting, squeezing in tight beside Chikanee, where he would settle down after giving a few deep sighs, vastly pleased, no doubt, with his day's work. And Sajo, not wishing to disturb them, would stay there until they were ready to go.

It was very easy to tell them apart by now, as they had become quite different in their ways. Chilawee was stronger, bolder and more adventurous than his chum, a kind of a comical fellow who seemed to enjoy bumping his head on the table-legs, or dropping things on his toes, or falling into the wood-box. He was as inquisitive as a parrot and wanted to be into everything, which he generally was, if he could reach it. Once he climbed up onto the edge of a pail of water that someone had left on the floor for a moment, and perhaps mistaking it for a plunge-hole, dived right into it. The pail, of course, upset with a bang, splashing the water in all directions. He was most surprised; and so was everybody else. But in spite of all this wilful behaviour, he was just as affectionate as Chikanee, and dogged Shapian's footsteps (when not otherwise engaged!) nearly as much as the other one did Sajo's. And he could not bear to be away from Chikanee very long. Everywhere they went they were together, trotting along one behind the other, or side by side, and if they should become parted on their wanderings in the camp, they would start out to look for each other, and call to one another. And when they met they would sit quite still for a little time, with their heads together, holding each other by the fur – though this wistful mood soon passed off, and it was not long before it all ended up in one of those queer wrestling matches, which seemed to be their way of celebrating.

And Sajo often thought how cruel it would be to ever part them.

Winter Dog

◄O►

ALISTAIR MACLEOD

Alistair MacLeod (b. 1936) is a Maritimer who teaches creative writing at the University of Windsor. He was born in North Battleford, Saskatchewan, but has lived mostly in Nova Scotia's Inverness County. His Celtic heritage permeates his literary imagination so that the history, folklore and experience of Scottish immigrants informs his narrator's voice, which can easily be mistaken for his own voice. He insists that his writing is not autobiographical; "it seems very autobiographical because I work hard to make it seem true." The hard facts of life are squarely faced with no escape into romanticism.

"Winter Dog" is framed by the narrator's present. A few days before Christmas in southwestern Ontario, a man waits for news of

a dying relative. The sight of his children playing in the snow with a golden collie-like dog sparks a childhood memory. The natural world of Cape Breton, where he grew up, was harsh and primitive, a place where boys had to face the dangers of storm and sea with courage, intelligence and determination, if they were to survive. A desire to salvage a seal from the off-shore ice had plunged the twelve-year-old and his dog into a condition of high risk – a favourite theme of the author. The account of the adventure is constructed so that each danger heightens the suspense. The story well illustrates the advice that MacLeod gives his students: "Write from the heart." A literary ancestor of the "dog-as-hero" type is Norman Duncan's Newfoundland tale, Billy Topsail and Co., *written almost a century earlier. "Winter Dog" appears in* As Birds Bring Forth the Sun *(1986). MacLeod has also written* The Lost Salt Gift of Blood *(1976) and* Island *(1989).*

◄○►

I am writing this in December. In the period close to Christmas, and three days after the first snowfall in this region of south-western Ontario. The snow came quietly in the night or in the early morning. When we went to bed near midnight, there was none at all. Then early in the morning we heard the children singing Christmas songs from their rooms across the hall. It was very dark and I rolled over to check the time. It was 4:30 a.m. One of them must have awakened and looked out the window to find the snow and then eagerly awakened the others. They are half crazed by the promise of Christmas, and the discovery of the snow is an unexpected giddy surprise. There was no snow promised for this area, not even yesterday.

"What are you doing?" I call, although it is obvious.

"Singing Christmas songs," they shout back with equal obviousness, "because it snowed."

"Try to be quiet," I say, "or you'll wake the baby."

"She's already awake," they say. "She's listening to our singing. She likes it. Can we go out and make a snowman?"

I roll from my bed and go to the window. The neighbouring houses are muffled in snow and silence and there are as yet no lights in any of them. The snow has stopped falling and its whitened quietness reflects the shadows of the night.

"This snow is no good for snowmen," I say. "It is too dry."

"How can snow be dry?" asks a young voice. Then an older one says, "Well, then can we go out and make the first tracks?"

They take my silence for consent and there are great sounds of rustling and giggling as they go downstairs to touch the light switches and rummage and jostle for coats and boots.

"What on earth is happening?" asks my wife from her bed. "What are they doing?"

"They are going outside to make the first tracks in the snow," I say. "It snowed quite heavily last night."

"What time is it?"

"Shortly after 4:30."

"Oh."

We ourselves have been nervous and restless for the past weeks. We have been troubled by illness and uncertainty in those we love far away on Canada's east coast. We have already considered and rejected driving the fifteen hundred miles. Too far, too uncertain, too expensive, fickle weather, the complications of transporting Santa Claus.

Instead, we sleep uncertainly and toss in unbidden dreams. We jump when the phone rings after 10:00 p.m. and are then reassured by the distant voices.

"First of all, there is nothing wrong," they say. "Things are just the same."

Sometimes we make calls ourselves, even to the hospital in Halifax, and are surprised at the voices which answer.

"I just got here this afternoon from Newfoundland. I'm going to try to stay a week. He seems better today. He's sleeping now."

At other times we receive calls from farther west, from Edmonton and Calgary and Vancouver. People hoping to find objectivity in the most subjective of situations. Strung out in uncertainty across the time zones from British Columbia to Newfoundland.

Within our present city, people move and consider possibilities:

If he dies tonight we'll leave right away. Can you come?

We will have to drive as we'll never get air reservations at this time.

I'm not sure if my car is good enough. I'm always afraid of the mountains near Cabano.

If we were stranded in Rivière du Loup we would be worse off than being here. It would be too far for anyone to come and get us.

My car will go but I'm not so sure I can drive it all the way. My eyes are not so good anymore, especially at night in drifting snow.

Perhaps there'll be no drifting snow.

There's always drifting snow.

We'll take my car if you'll drive it. We'll have to drive straight through.

John phoned and said he'll give us his car if we want it or he'll drive – either his own car or someone else's.

He drinks too heavily, especially for long-distance driving, and at this time of year. He's been drinking ever since this news began.

He drinks because he cares. It's just the way he is.

Not everybody drinks.

Not everybody cares, and if he gives you his word, he'll never drink until he gets there. We all know that.

But so far nothing has happened. Things seem to remain the same.

Through the window and out on the white plane of the snow, the silent, laughing children now appear. They move in their muffled clothes like mummers on the whitest of stages. They dance and gesture noiselessly, flopping their arms in parodies of heavy, happy, earthbound birds. They have been warned by the eldest to be aware of the sleeping neighbours so they cavort only in panto-mime, sometimes raising mittened hands to their mouths to suppress their joyous laughter. They dance and prance in the moonlight, tossing snow in one another's direction, tracing out various shapes and initials, forming lines which snake across the previously unmarked whiteness. All of it in silence, unknown and unseen and unheard to the neighbouring world. They seem unreal even to me, their father, standing at his darkened window. It is almost as if they have danced out of the world of folklore like happy elves who cavort and mimic and caper through the private hours of this whitened dark, only to vanish with the coming of the morning's light and leaving only the signs of their activities behind.

I am tempted to check the recently vacated beds to confirm what perhaps I think I know.

Then out of the corner of my eye I see him. The golden collie-like dog. He appears almost as if from the wings of the stage or as a figure newly noticed in the lower corner of a winter painting. He sits quietly and watches the playful scene before him and then, as if responding to a silent invitation, bounds into its midst. The children chase him in frantic circles, falling and rolling as he doubles back and darts and dodges between their legs and through their outstretched arms. He seizes a mitt loosened from its owner's hand, and tosses it happily in the air and then snatches it back into his jaws an instant before it reaches the ground and seconds before the tumbling bodies fall on the emptiness of its expected destination. He races to the edge of the scene and lies facing them, holding the mitt tantalizingly between his paws, and then as they dash towards him, he leaps forward again, tossing and catching it before him and zigzagging through them as the Sunday football player might return the much sought-after ball. After he has gone through and eluded them all, he looks back over his shoulder and again, like an elated athlete, tosses the mitt high in what seems like an imaginary end zone. Then he seizes it once more and lopes in a wide circle around his pursuers, eventually coming closer and closer to them until once more their stretching hands are able to actually touch his shoulders and back and haunches, although he continues always to wriggle free. He is touched but never captured, which is the nature of the game. Then he is gone. As suddenly as he came. I strain my eyes in the direction of the adjoining street, towards the house where I have often seen him, always within a yard enclosed by woven links of chain. I see the flash of his silhouette, outlined perhaps against the snow or the light cast by the street lamps or the moon. It arcs upwards and seems to hang for an instant high above the top of the fence and then it descends on the other side. He lands on his shoulder in a fluff of snow and with a half roll regains his feet and vanishes within the shadow of his owner's house.

"What are you looking at?" asks my wife.

"That golden collie-like dog from the other street was just playing with the children in the snow."

"But he's always in that fenced-in yard."

"I guess not always. He jumped the fence just now and went back in. I guess the owners and the rest of us think he's fenced in but he knows he's not. He probably comes out every night and leads an exciting life. I hope they don't see his tracks or they'll probably begin to chain him."

"What are the children doing?"

"They look tired now from chasing the dog. They'll probably soon be back in. I think I'll go downstairs and wait for them and make myself a cup of coffee."

"Okay."

I look once more towards the fenced-in yard but the dog is nowhere to be seen.

I first saw such a dog when I was twelve and he came as a pup of about two months in a crate to the railroad station which was about eight miles from where we lived. Someone must have phoned or dropped in to say: "Your dog's at the station."

He had come to Cape Breton in response to a letter and a cheque which my father had sent to Morrisburg, Ontario. We had seen the ads for "cattle collie dogs" in the *Family Herald*, which was the farm newspaper of the time, and we were in need of a good young working dog.

His crate was clean and neat and there was still a supply of dog biscuits with him and a can in the corner to hold water. The baggage handlers had looked after him well on the trip east, and he appeared in good spirits. He had a white collar and chest and four rather large white paws and a small white blaze on his fore-head. The rest of him was a fluffy, golden brown, although his eyebrows and the tips of his ears as well as the end of his tail were darker, tingeing almost to black. When he grew to his full size the blackish shadings became really black, and although he had the long, heavy coat of a collie, it was in certain areas more grey than gold. He was also taller than the average collie and with a deeper chest. He seemed to be at least part German Shepherd.

It was winter when he came and we kept him in the house where he slept behind the stove in a box lined with an old coat. Our other dogs slept mostly in the stables or outside in the lees of woodpiles or under porches or curled up on the banking of the house. We seemed to care more for him because he was smaller and it was winter and he was somehow like a visitor; and also because more was expected of him and also perhaps because we had paid money for him and thought about his coming for some time – like a "planned" child. Sceptical neighbours and relatives who thought the idea of paying money for a dog was rather exotic or frivolous would ask: "Is that your Ontario dog" or "Do you think your Ontario dog will be any good?"

He turned out to be no good at all and no one knew why. Perhaps it was because of the suspected German Shepherd blood. But he could not "get the hang of it." Although we worked him and trained him as we had other dogs, he seemed always to bring panic instead of order and to make things worse instead of better. He became a "head dog," which meant that instead of working behind the cattle he lunged at their heads, impeding them from any forward motion and causing them to turn in endless, meaningless bewildered circles. On the few occasions when he did go behind them, he was "rough," which meant that instead of being a floating, nipping, suggestive presence, he actually bit them and caused them to gallop, which was another sin. Sometimes in the summer the milk cows suffering from his misunderstood pursuit would jam pell mell into the stable, tossing their wide horns in fear, and with their great sides heaving and perspiring while down their legs and tails the wasted milk ran in rivulets mingling with the blood caused by his slashing wounds. He was, it was said, "worse than nothing."

Gradually everyone despaired, although he continued to grow grey and golden and was, as everyone agreed, a "beautiful-looking dog."

He was also tremendously strong and in the winter months I would hitch him to a sleigh which he pulled easily and willingly on almost any kind of surface. When he was harnessed I used to put a collar around his neck and attach a light line to it so that I might have some minimum control over him, but it was hardly ever needed. He would pull home the Christmas tree or the bag of flour or the deer which was shot far back in the woods; and when we visited our winter snares he would pull home the gunnysacks which contained the partridges and rabbits which we gathered. He would also pull us, especially on the flat windswept stretches of land beside the sea. There the snow was never really deep and the water that oozed from a series of fresh-water springs and ponds contributed to a glaze of ice and crisply crusted snow which the sleigh runners seemed to sing over without ever breaking through. He would begin with an easy lope and then increase his swiftness until both he and the sleigh seemed to touch the surface at only irregular intervals. He would stretch out then with his ears flattened against his head and his shoulders bunching and contracting in the rhythm of his speed. Behind him on the sleigh we would cling tenaciously to the wooden slats as the particles of ice and snow dislodged by his nails hurtled towards our faces. We would avert our heads and close our eyes and the wind stung so sharply that the difference between freezing and burning could not be known. He would do that until late in the afternoon when it was time to return home and begin our chores.

On the sunny winter Sunday that I am thinking of, I planned to visit my snares. There seemed no other children around that afternoon and the adults were expecting relatives. I harnessed the dog to the sleigh, opened the door of the house and shouted that I was going to look at my snares. We began to climb the hill behind the house on our way to the woods when we looked back and out towards the sea. The "big ice," which was what we called the major pack of drift ice, was in solidly against the shore and stretched out beyond the range of vision. It had not been "in" yesterday, although for the past weeks we had seen it moving offshore, sometimes close and sometimes distant, depending on the winds and tides. The coming of the big ice marked the official beginning of the coldest part of winter. It was mostly drift ice from the Arctic and Labrador, although some of it was fresh-water ice from the estuary of the St. Lawrence. It drifted down with the dropping temperatures, bringing its own mysterious coldness and stretching for hundreds of miles in craters and pans, sometimes in grotesque shapes and sometimes in dazzling architectural forms. It was blue and white and sometimes grey and at other times a dazzling emerald green.

The dog and I changed our direction towards the sea, to find what the ice might yield. Our land had always been beside the sea and we had always gone towards it to find newness and the extraordinary; and over the years we, as others along the coast, had found quite a lot, although never the pirate chests of gold which were supposed to abound or the reasons for the mysterious lights that our elders still spoke of and persisted in seeing. But kegs of rum had washed up, and sometimes bloated horses and various fishing paraphernalia and valuable timber and furniture from foundered ships. The door of my room was apparently the galley door from a ship called the *Judith Franklin* which was wrecked during the early winter in which my great-grandfather was building his house. My grandfather told of how they had heard the cries and seen the lights as the ship neared the rocks and of how they had run down in the dark and tossed lines to the people while tying themselves to trees on the shore. All were saved, including women clinging to small children. The next day the builders of the new house went down to the shore and salvaged what they could from the wreckage of the vanquished ship. A sort of symbolic marriage of the new and the old: doors and shelving, stairways, hatches, wooden chests and trunks and various glass figurines and lanterns which were miraculously never broken.

People came too. The dead as well as the living. Bodies of men swept overboard and reported lost at sea and the bodies of men still crouched within the shelter of their boats' broken bows. And sometimes in late winter young sealers who had quit their vessels would walk across the ice and come to our doors. They were usually very young – some still in their teens – and had signed on for jobs they could not or no longer wished to handle. They were often disoriented and did not know where they were, only that they had seen land and had decided to walk towards it. They were often frostbitten and with little money and uncertain as to how they might get to Halifax. The dog and I walked towards the ice upon the sea.

Sometimes it was hard to "get on" the ice, which meant that at the point where the pack met the shore there might be open water or irregularities caused by the indentations of the coastline or the workings of the tides and currents, but for us on that day there was no difficulty at all. We were "on" easily and effortlessly and enthused in our new adventure. For the first mile there was nothing but the vastness of the white expanse. We came to a clear stretch where the ice was as smooth and unruffled as that of an indoor arena and I knelt on the sleigh while the dog loped easily along. Gradually the ice changed to an uneven terrain of pressure ridges and hummocks, making it impossible to ride farther; and then suddenly, upon rounding a hummock, I saw the perfect seal. At first I thought it was alive, as did the dog who stopped so suddenly in his tracks that the sleigh almost collided with his legs. The hackles on the back of his neck rose and he growled in the danger-ous way he was beginning to develop. But the seal was dead, yet facing us in a frozen perfection that was difficult to believe. There was a light powder of snow over its darker coat and a delicate rime of frost still formed the outline of its whiskers. Its eyes were wide open and it stared straight ahead towards the land. Even now in memory it seems more real than reality – as if it were transformed by frozen art into something more arresting than life itself. The way the sudden seal in the museum exhibit freezes your eyes with the touch of truth. Immediately I wanted to take it home.

It was frozen solidly in a base of ice so I began to look for something that might serve as a pry. I let the dog out of his harness and hung the sleigh and harness on top of the hummock to mark the place and began my search. Some distance away I found a pole about twelve feet long. It is always surprising to find such things on the ice field but they are, often amazingly, there, almost in the same way that you might find a pole floating in the summer ocean. Unpredictable but possible. I took the pole back and began my work. The dog went off on explorations of his own.

Although it was firmly frozen, the task did not seem impossible and by inserting the end of the pole under first one side and then the other and working from the front to the back, it was possible to cause a gradual loosening. I remember thinking how very warm it was because I was working hard and perspiring heavily. When the dog came back he was uneasy, and I realized it was starting to snow a bit but I was almost done. He sniffed with disinterest at the seal and began to whine a bit, which was something he did not often do. Finally, after another quarter of an hour, I was able to roll my trophy onto the sleigh and with the dog in harness we set off. We had gone perhaps two hundred yards when the seal slid free. I took the dog and the sleigh back and once again managed to roll the seal on. This time I took the line from the dog's collar and tied the seal to the sleigh, reasoning that the dog would go home anyway and there would be no need to guide him. My fingers were numb as I tried to fasten the awkward knots and the dog began to whine and rear. When I gave the command he bolted forward and I clung at the back of the sleigh to the seal. The snow was heavier now and blowing in my face but we were moving rapidly and when we came to the stretch of arena-like ice we skimmed across it almost like an iceboat, the profile of the frozen seal at the front of the sleigh like those figures at the prows of Viking ships. At the very end of the smooth stretch, we went through. From my position at the end of the sleigh I felt him drop almost before I saw him, and rolled backwards seconds before the sleigh and seal followed him into the blackness of the water. He went under once carried by his own momentum but surfaced almost immediately with his head up and his paws scrambling at the icy, jagged edge of the hole; but when the weight and momentum of the sleigh and its burden struck, he went down again, this time out of sight.

I realized we had struck a "seam" and that the stretch of smooth ice had been deceivingly and temporarily joined to the rougher ice near the shore and now was in the process of breaking away. I saw the widening line before me and jumped to the other side just as his head miraculously came up once more. I lay on my stomach and grabbed his collar in both my hands and then in a moment of panic did not know what to do. I could feel myself sliding towards him and the darkness of the water and was aware of the weight that pulled me forward and down. I was also aware of his razor-sharp claws flailing violently before my face and knew that I might lose my eyes. And I was aware that his own eyes were bulging from their sockets and that he might think I was trying to choke him and might lunge and slash my face with his teeth in desperation. I knew all of this but somehow did nothing about it; it seemed almost simpler to hang on and be drawn into the darkness of the gently slopping water, seeming to slop gently in spite of all the agitation. Then suddenly he was free, scrambling over my shoulder and dragging the sleigh behind him. The seal surfaced again, buoyed up perhaps by the physics of its frozen body or the nature of its fur. Still looking more genuine than it could have in life, its snout and head broke the open water and it seemed to look at us curiously for an instant before it vanished permanently beneath the ice. The loose and badly tied knots had apparently not held when the sleigh was in a near-vertical position and we were saved by the ineptitude of my own numbed fingers. We had been spared for a future time.

He lay gasping and choking for a moment, coughing up the icy salt water, and then almost immediately his coat began to freeze. I realized then how cold I was myself and that even in the moments I had been lying on the ice, my clothes had begun to adhere to it. My earlier heated perspiration was now a cold rime upon my body and I imagined it outlining me there, beneath my clothes, in a sketch of frosty white. I got on the sleigh once more and crouched low as he began to race towards home. His coat was freezing fast, and as he ran the individual ice-coated hairs began to clack together like rhythmical castanets attuned to the motion of his body. It was snowing quite heavily in our faces now and it seemed to be approaching dusk, although I doubted if it were so on the land which I could now no longer see. I realized all the obvious things I should have considered earlier. That if the snow was blowing in our faces, the wind was off the land, and if it was off the land, it was blowing the ice pack back out to sea. That was probably one reason why the seam had opened. And also that the ice had only been "in" one night and had not had a chance to "set." I

realized other things as well. That it was the time of the late afternoon when the tide was falling. That no one knew where we were.
That I had said we were going to look at snares, which was not
where we had gone at all. And I remembered now that I had
received no answer even to that misinformation, so perhaps I
had not even been heard. And also if there was drifting snow like
this on land, our tracks would by now have been obliterated.

We came to a rough section of ice: huge slabs on their sides and
others piled one on top of the other as if they were in some strange
form of storage. It was no longer possible to ride the sleigh but as
I stood up I lifted it and hung on to it as a means of holding on to
the dog. The line usually attached to his collar had sunk with the
vanished seal. My knees were stiff when I stood up; and deprived
of the windbreak effect which the dog had provided, I felt the
snow driving full into my face, particularly my eyes. It did not
merely impede my vision, the way distant snow flurries might, but
actually entered my eyes, causing them to water and freeze nearly
shut. I was aware of the weight of ice on my eyelashes and could
see them as they gradually lowered and became heavier. I did not
remember ice like this when I got on, although I did not find that
terribly surprising. I pressed the soles of my numbed feet firmly
down upon it to try and feel if it was moving out, but it was impossible to tell because there was no fixed point of reference. Almost
the sensation one gets on a conveyor belt at airports or on escala-
tors; although you are standing still you recognize motion, but
should you shut your eyes and be deprived of sight, even that
recognition may become ambiguously uncertain.

The dog began to whine and to walk around me in circles,
binding my legs with the traces of the harness as I continued to

grasp the sleigh. Finally I decided to let him go as there seemed no way to hold him and there was nothing else to do. I unhitched the traces and doubled them up as best I could and tucked them under the backpad of his harness so they would not drag behind him and become snagged on any obstacles. I did not take off my mitts to do so as I was afraid I would not be able to get them back on. He vanished into the snow almost immediately.

The sleigh had been a gift from an uncle, so I hung on to it and carried it with both hands before me like an ineffectual shield against the wind and snow. I lowered my head as much as I could and turned it sideways so the wind would beat against my head instead of directly into my face. Sometimes I would turn and walk backwards for a few steps. Although I knew it was not the wisest thing to do, it seemed at times the only way to breathe. And then I began to feel the water sloshing about my feet.

Sometimes when the tides or currents ran heavily and the ice began to separate, the water that was beneath it would well up and wash over it almost as if it were reflooding it. Sometimes you could see the hard ice clearly beneath the water but at other times a sort of floating slush was formed mingling with snow and "slob" ice which was not yet solid. It was thick and dense and soupy and it was impossible to see what lay beneath it. Experienced men on the ice sometimes carried a slender pole so they could test the consistency of the footing which might or might not lie before them, but I was obviously not one of them, although I had a momentary twinge for the pole I had used to dislodge the seal. Still, there was nothing to do but go forward.

When I went through, the first sensation was almost of relief and relaxation for the water initially made me feel much warmer than I had been on the surface. It was the most dangerous of false sensations for I knew my clothes were becoming heavier by the second. I clung to the sleigh somewhat as a raft and lunged forward with it in a kind of up-and-down swimming motion, hoping that it might strike some sort of solidity before my arms became so weighted and sodden that I could no longer lift them. I cried out then for the first time into the driving snow.

He came almost immediately, although I could see he was afraid and the slobbing slush was up to his knees. Still, he seemed to be on some kind of solid footing for he was not swimming. I splashed towards him and when almost there, desperately threw the sleigh before me and lunged for the edge of what seemed like his footing, but it only gave way as if my hands were closing on icy insubstantial porridge. He moved forward then, although I still could not tell if what supported him would be of any use to me. Finally I grasped the breast strap of his harness. He began to back up then, and as I said, he was tremendously strong. The harness began to slide forward on his shoulders but he continued to pull as I continued to grasp and then I could feel my elbows on what seemed like solid ice and I was able to hook them on the edge and draw myself, dripping and soaking, like another seal out of the black water and onto the whiteness of the slushy ice. Almost at once my clothes began to freeze. My elbows and knees began to creak when I bent them as if I were a robot from the realm of science fiction and then I could see myself clothed in transparent ice as if I had been coated with shellac or finished with clear varnish.

As the fall into the winter sea had at first seemed ironically warm, so now my garments of ice seemed a protection against the biting wind, but I knew it was a deceptive sensation and that I did not have much time before me. The dog faced into the wind and I followed him. This time he stayed in sight, and at times even turned back to wait for me. He was cautious but certain and gradually the slush disappeared, and although we were still in water, the ice was hard and clear beneath it. The frozen heaviness of my clothes began to weigh on me and I could feel myself, ironically, perspiring within my suit of icy armour. I was very tired, which I knew was another dangerous sensation. And then I saw the land. It was very close and a sudden surprise. Almost like coming upon a stalled and unexpected automobile in a highway's winter storm. It was only yards away, and although there was no longer any ice actually touching the shore, there were several pans of it floating in the region between. The dog jumped from one to the other and I followed him, still clutching the sleigh, and missing only the last pan which floated close to the rocky shore. The water came only to my waist and I was able to touch the bottom and splash noisily on land. We had been spared again for a future time and I was never to know whether he had reached the shore himself and come back or whether he had heard my call against the wind.

We began to run towards home and the land lightened and there were touches of evening sun. The wind still blew but no snow was falling. Yet when I looked back, the ice and the ocean were invisible in the swirling squalls. It was like looking at another far and distant country on the screen of a snowy television.

I became obsessed, now that I could afford the luxury, with not being found disobedient or considered a fool. The visitors' vehicles were still in the yard so I imagined most of the family to be in the parlour or living room, and I circled the house and entered through the kitchen, taking the dog with me. I was able to get upstairs unnoticed and get my clothes changed and when I came down I mingled with everybody and tried to appear as normal as I could. My own family was caught up with the visitors and only general comments came my way. The dog, who could not change his clothes, lay under the table with his head on his paws and he was also largely unnoticed. Later as the ice melted from his coat, a puddle formed around him, which I casually mopped up. Still later someone said, "I wonder where that dog has been, his coat is soaking wet." I was never to tell anyone of the afternoon's experience or that he had saved my life.

Two winters later I was sitting at a neighbour's kitchen table when I looked out the window and saw the dog as he was shot. He had followed my father and also me and had been sitting rather regally on a little hill beside the house and I suppose had presented an ideal target. But he had moved at just the right or wrong time and instead of killing him the high-powered bullet smashed into his shoulder. He jumped into the air and turned his snapping teeth upon the wound, trying to bite the cause of the pain he could not see. And then he turned towards home, unsteady but still strong on his three remaining legs. No doubt he felt, as we all do, that if he could get home he might be saved, but he did not make it, as we knew he could not, because of the amount of blood on the snow and the wavering pattern of his three-legged tracks. Yet he was, as I said, tremendously strong and he managed almost three-quarters of a mile. The house he sought must have been within his vision when he died for we could see it quite clearly when we came to his body by the roadside. His eyes were open and his tongue was clenched between his teeth and the little blood he had left dropped red and black on the winter snow. He was not to be saved for a future time anymore.

I learned later that my father had asked the neighbour to shoot him and that we had led him into a kind of ambush. Perhaps my father did so because the neighbour was younger and had a better gun or was a better shot. Perhaps because my father did not want to be involved. It was obvious he had not planned on things turning out so messy.

The dog had become increasingly powerful and protective, to the extent that people were afraid to come into the yard. And he had also bitten two of the neighbour's children and caused them to be frightened of passing our house on their journeys to and from school. And perhaps there was also the feeling in the community that he was getting more than his share of the breeding: that he travelled farther than other dogs on his nightly forays and that he fought off and injured the other smaller dogs who might compete with him for female favours. Perhaps there was fear that his dominance and undesirable characteristics did not bode well for future generations.

This has been the writing down of a memory triggered by the sight of a golden dog at play in the silent snow with my own excited children. After they came in and had their hot chocolate, the wind began to blow; and by the time I left for work, there was no evidence of their early-morning revels or any dog tracks leading to the chain-link fence. The "enclosed" dog looked impassively at me as I brushed the snow from the buried windshield. What does he know? he seemed to say.

The snow continues to drift and to persist as another uncertainty added to those we already have. Should we be forced to drive tonight, it will be a long, tough journey into the wind and the driving snow which is pounding across Ontario and Quebec and New Brunswick and against the granite coast of Nova Scotia. Should we be drawn by death, we might well meet our own. Still, it is only because I am alive that I can even consider such possibilities. Had I not been saved by the golden dog, I would not have these tight concerns or children playing in the snow or of course these memories. It is because of him that I have been able to come this far in time.

It is too bad that I could not have saved him as well and my feelings did him little good as I looked upon his bloodied body there beside the road. It was too late and out of my control and even if I had known the possibilities of the future it would not have been easy.

He was with us only for a while and brought his own changes, and yet he still persists. He persists in my memory and in my life and he persists physically as well. He is there in this winter storm. There in the golden-grey dogs with their black-tipped ears and tails, sleeping in the stables or in the lees of woodpiles or under porches or curled beside the houses which face towards the sea.

Woo's Life

◄o►

EMILY CARR

*Emily Carr (1871-1945) was an important Canadian artist whose
work was largely derided or ignored during her lifetime. Born in
Victoria, British Columbia, she trained at art schools in San
Francisco, London and Paris. Her profession was so unremunera-
tive that she had to supplement her income by operating a boarding
house in Victoria, making pottery and hooked rugs and raising
dogs. Her relationships with people, including her sisters, her
tenants and the curators of art galleries and museums, were often
strained. For reciprocal affection and loyalty she relied on her
animals – numerous dogs (usually griffons), Susie the white rat,
Joseph (one of many budgerigars), Sallie, a white cockatoo, Jane
the talking parrot, monkeys, English doves, canaries. "Thank the*

Lord for dogs, white rats and monkeys," she confided to her journal. "They, at least, are stable. Their love springs don't dry up but bubble on and on right to the grave and after."

Perhaps the best loved and certainly the most interesting of the pets was a Javanese monkey acquired in the early 1920s and surrendered to Vancouver's Stanley Park Zoo in 1937, when Carr's health became precarious. In Emily Carr as I Knew Her (1954), Carol Pearson provides an engaging word portrait of Woo that supplements Carr's writing – Woo shaking the parrots' cage to get them yelling; draining cups after a tea party and leaving each cup upside down in its saucer; answering the telephone then letting Jane the talking parrot loose to yell into the mouthpiece "Hello," "Who else?" and "Speak up, speak up!" The monkey's uninhibited delight in mischief-making was one of her most endearing qualities. It was as if, regarded as an "inferior being" by conventional society, she could indulge in a degree of irresponsibility denied to her mistress. "Portrait of Woo," a painting in the collection of the Provincial Archives in Victoria (reproduced in Hundreds and Thousands: The Journals of Emily Carr), shows the monkey, looking remarkably like a little girl in her tawny-coloured hoop style dress with its enormous yellow bow. Her feet planted firmly on a lower branch and her hands grasping a higher one, she gazes into space, intently and curiously.

When a serious heart condition made it difficult and dangerous for Carr to spend long periods sketching and painting the isolated Indian villages and thick rainforests of the British Columbia coast, she turned to writing. "I am trying to write some animal stories but find them appallingly difficult, even a cow wouldn't want to read them," she confided to a Vancouver friend, Nan Cheney

December 14, 1931). By March 1938, she was acknowledging, again to Cheney, that "I feel more 'writing' than 'painting' these days, and it makes me feel 'blisterish' . . . . I feel, I should be paint-ing not wasting my time trying to scribble at my age." One of those who encouraged her "scribbling" was Dr. G.G. Sedgewick, Head of the University of British Columbia's Department of English. It was Sedgewick who gave Carr's stories their first expo-sure by reading them on the CBC in 1940 and by urging their publication. Klee Wyck *was published in 1942, followed by* The Book of Small *(1942),* The House of All Sorts *(1945), and* The Heart of a Peacock *(1953).*

—<o>—

*I*have not tried to write a book of funny monkey stories, the *aimless, helter-skelter ways that appear to be common to monkeys. I have tried to show the apparent reaction of my partic-ular monkey to domestic life and to humans and the reaction of humans and domestic creatures to Woo, my small Javanese who lived under close, loving observation in my home for thirteen of the fifteen years of her life.*

Buying Woo

The pet shop owner thought the apex of her troubles was reached in the Customs; now that the shipment was cleared, the crates standing in the centre of the pet shop floor, she realized that this was not so – there were the monkeys! From the pile of boxes and cages on the floor came mews, squawks, grunts – protests of creatures travel-worn and restless. If a crate was quite still, things were bad.

Finches, canaries, love-birds, parrots, Siamese cats, squirrels, and, at the bottom of the pile, monkeys, gibbering, beating their fists upon the sides of crates demanding immediate release.

"You monks must wait," said the weary woman wondering how their bedlam was to be endured. "Your cage is not ready." However, as makeshift she rolled an empty barrel from somewhere, nailed a heavy wire parrot cage over its top and manoeuvred the monkeys from crate to barrel. Two fair-sized monkeys rushed up into the cage, delighted with release from cramping dark, squeaking, thrusting hairy arms through the bars, grabbing hammer, nails, packets of bird seed, the tail of a bantam rooster – anything that could be reached. I, waiting to buy bird-seed, saw a tiny little black face pop from the dark of the barrel to be immediately pushed down by the heavy hind foot of one of the big monkeys. Time and again the little face, a tuft of surprised Kewpie hair peaked on the top of its baby head, tried to get a peep at its new environment, only to be forced back like a jack into its box.

The pathetic little face haunted me. Going to sleep I thought about it and in the night when I woke.

When morning came I went to the phone calling the pet shop.

"Is that tiny monkey boy or girl?"

"Girl."

Suddenly I wanted her – I wanted her *tremendously*. Of course, I wasn't going to buy a monkey, but I asked, "What is her price?"

My voice went squeaky with wanting. The woman understood: she had heard that "wanting squeak" before.

"Buy her. She is a *very* nice monkey and the big ones bully her."

"But my family! If I paid so much money for a monkey!"

"Listen, everyone is entitled to some fun. Would you consider even trade for one of your griffon pups?" (She knew my kennel.)

Good luck forever to that understanding woman! The deal was made. She would sell a "griff" quicker than a monk.

Pearl, my kitchen maid, loved animals as I did. I told her first.

"A real monkey, glory be! How soon can I fetch it?" Within an hour Pearl was racing down the street carrying a small parrot's travelling cage and bursting with excitement.

I heard them coming up the stairs just as we sat down to lunch – my sister Lizzie, a man whom we boarded, and I. Pearl's face was absolutely apoplectic. She placed the cage upon the floor.

Dead silence! My sister's eyes popped like a Peke dog's.

"Woo!" announced a plaintive voice from the cage. "Woo, woo, woo!"

"Your new niece, Lizzie!" I said, brave in the knowledge that my home was my own, yet half scared of family criticism.

My sister pushed aside her soup. "Milly! I never, never, *never* thought a relative of mine would sink to a – a – a baboon!"

The boarder's lips always leaked when he ate soup. In the intensity of his stare he entirely forgot his serviette. Soup splashed from his spoon back into his plate, plop!

"Er, er, er, er!" (Ordinarily he said "Er" only twice to climb to each sentence.)

"Er – er – er – er it's a monkey!"

The monkey decided to investigate us. Sticking one hand and one foot out of each side of the narrow cage she propelled herself across the floor. A walking cage looked so comical that a laugh even squeezed out of Lizzie – she cut it short with, "How much did you pay for the preposterous creature?"

"Even trade for a griffon pup."

"A griffon! The idea!"

You'd have thought that I had traded a diamond necklace for an apple, though Lizzie always *pretended* to despise my little dogs.

"Your house will smell! Everything in it will be smashed! Your friends will drop away – who wants to 'hob-nob' with a monkey!" This awful fate trailed back at me as sister Lizzie rushed down my stair returning to her own chaste house and leaving me to contemplate the wreck I had made of my life.

The boarder, who set great store on the "griffon dogs," groaned, "Er – er, a griffon for a monkey!" and went off to his office.

Pearl and I sat on the floor thrilled by the absorbing strangeness of our new creature.

My sister Alice took the first opportunity to come from her house round the corner to inspect my new queerness.

"Everyone to his own taste," she shrugged. "Monkeys are *not* mine."

So Woo was introduced to my sisters and took her place in our family circle, no more a commercial commodity, but an element pertaining to the family life of the three Carr sisters.

Pearl and I spent that afternoon nibbling around the edge of something unknown to us. I had tamed squirrels, crows, coons, even a vulture – these creatures, like myself, were northern bred. This lightning-quick, temperamental, tropical thing belonged to a different country, different zone, different hemisphere. We were ignorant as to what liberties we dare take. If thwarted, Woo opened her mouth, exhibiting magnificent jaws of strong white teeth, jaws so wide-hinged that you could see her wisdoms (if she had any) and right down her throat. The boarder asked nervously, "Er – er – was it King Something or his son that died of monkey bite?"

I put the monkey into a large parrot cage. She snatched ungraciously all that we offered, food or play-things, grimacing back at us. When night fell she began to miss the warmth of the other monkeys, for though they had tormented her by day, they had been willing to pool cuddles at night. "Woo, woo, woo," she cried, and could find no comfort in the hot brick I offered or in Pearl's old sweater or in the boarder's third-best hat.

"Er – er – tell her to curl up in the hat. Er – er – it's a good hat."

He said this as if I were a monkey interpreter. But I had no monkey word to comfort the lonely little beast other than to repeat her own sad wailing, "Woo, woo, woo."

I had intended to call my monkey Jemima, but she named herself Woo that first night and Woo she remained for life.

Near midnight, she rolled herself up in Pearl's sweater and slept. I turned out the light, tiptoed from the room. A jungle stranger had possession of the studio.

Even restricted in a cage she was a foreign, undomestic note in my humdrum house!

There was a small collar on Woo's neck when I bought her. She had never known the pull of a chain. Any restraint, any touch of her collar infuriated her. By keeping a few links of chain always suspended from her neck I soon accustomed her to lead. Then I could take her into the garden.

Woo was teachable. Before I had owned her a week she got away from her chain in the garden.

"Good-bye, Woo!"

I was sad. I thought, of course, she would make for the woods in the Park nearby. No, Woo dashed up my stair, sat waiting on the mat to be let in. She had accepted the studio as her home. That quick response of love and trust entirely won me.

Woo's Appearance

Woo was probably under two years old when I got her. Trim, alert, dainty, her actions were smart and quick, her coat shone with health – she kept her greeny-brown coat immaculate.

Woo's hazel eyes were set close together and shadowed by bushy brows growing on a prominent ridge of bone – brows which were capable of wide movement, jumping up on her forehead or scowling down over creamy white eyelids which she lowered if humans stared directly at her. Monkeys only give stare for stare when their anger is roused; then a blazing fury burns fiercely at their opponent. The whites of Woo's eyes were dark brown, the irises clear and golden. The palms of hands and feet smooth, soft and black. Her small pointed face was black with a long, flat nose, wide, thin nostrils dilating when she was angry or excited. A fluff of whisker trimmed each cheek. Clean-eyed, clean-nosed, clean-mouthed, Woo washed her face as a cat washes, but, instead of the inner side of a velvet paw, she used the back of a doubled-up fist as a wash rag. She was very neat about her hands, licking them, scolding at any grease or stickiness, using grass, leaves or pinafore to clean them on.

This reminds me of Woo's clothing. Monkeys are liable to T.B. in our climate. I wanted to keep Woo out in the open as long as possible. I decided, therefore, when she began to shiver that I must make Woo some clothes. My first attempt was a dress of soft blue flannel. I fashioned it like a doll's dress. Woo was no stuffed dummy. The moment my back was turned she ripped the flannel dress to shreds – nothing was left but the collar-band.

"Flannel is apparently unsuitable," I remarked to Pearl.

"You did not allow enough straddle."

Pearl was right. My next attempt was short – wide, as a ballet skirt. Made of stout tweed coating, it had short sleeves. Woo chewed the woollen material into holes, so I made little flaring red duck aprons that she could not rip. These, over her warm tweeds, were cosy. Bobbing around my garden, she looked like a poinsettia bloom. She chewed off all buttons, undid hooks. So I buckled her garments at neck and waist.

Crows and robins visiting my cherry tree found one scare-crow that was no sham. The cherries beyond reach were Woo's. She sat on the tree-top – a queen. Amazed crow, baffled robin sat on the fence consulting.

Sewing

I sat by the Studio fire patching one of Woo's dresses; the dogs and monkey were sprawled round, sleeping. Woo sat up, stretched first one leg and then the other, yawned – every hair on her body stood at attention; she shook a great shake, beginning at her nose and ending at tail-tip. When every vibrating hair had settled into sleek oneness again, she jumped to the arm of my chair and scrutinized the needle going in and out of the cloth. "Woo," she murmured. "Woo, woo."

"Want to sew?" I handed her a pin and a piece of rag. Woo pushed the pin through the cloth; the head stuck each time. Angrily she tossed away pin and rag. I left the room for a moment. Woo was slipping from the table as I reentered. In her hand was the needle with which I had been sewing and which I had stuck into the pin-cushion on leaving the room. It was the only needle in a cushion full of pins. Woo picked up her rag, began to sew, each time painstakingly drawing the needle right through the cloth, sometimes helping it with her teeth, but always bringing it out on the opposite side to the one on which it went in. She would *not tolerate* thread in her needle: it snarled.

For several weeks Woo's favourite occupation was sewing. It absorbed her for an hour at a time. Suddenly she tired, threw away needle and rag, finished with needle-craft for good. That was Woo's way.

For the sake of variety I sometimes chained Woo to some movable object that she might wander round the garden and hunt insects. The article must be bulky enough that she could not lug it up the Studio stairs – Woo's one desire was always to get into my Studio.

One day I fastened her to a lumbering chair of wood. The chair was heavy and bulky. After proving that the cumbersome thing could not be got up the stair, Woo sat and thought. At the far end of the garden was a loaded apple tree – red, juicy apples. Woo had all the apples she could eat. It was not the fruit she wanted, but the pips at the core. She would destroy dozens of apples simply to get their seeds. She began tugging the chair, intent on reaching that best apple tree. She pulled, she pushed; the chair legs stuck in the grass roots. Then she tried heaving the chair over and over. Had she been able to steer straight, each flop would have brought the chair one length nearer to her goal; but the old chair flopped this direction and that. The tugging, grunting monkey paused every little while to eat an earwig. After a long, long struggle the chair toppled under the tree. Woo sprang, only to find that her chain would not allow her to climb out to the end of the boughs where the apples clustered.

No gallant serpent being in my garden to hand apples to little Eves, Woo got down, over and over went the chair till at last it was directly under the fruit, the chair on its side. It was still too low for her to reach the apples. She stood the chair upright, climbed the seat, climbed the back, reached for the biggest apple – too big for her hands, it dropped at touch, bumped Woo's head.

"Ooo-ooo-ooo!" She caught the fruit before it rolled beyond reach, gripped it in both wide-spread feet and burrowed for pips.

I saw with amazement my monkey's perseverance again. One sketching trip, I hired a cottage high up a steep bank. I took dogs and monkey to the beach while I worked, fastening Woo's chain to a derelict preserving kettle which I found among the drift. Soon the monkey tired of dabbling in the puddles. Her brain connected my being on the beach with the cottage being empty and the joy of rummaging unchecked.

She began lugging the great kettle over a wide stretch of drift between sand and bank. Mounting each log laboriously she hauled the kettle up on her chain, hand over hand like a sailor. She took it over dozens of separate logs, at last coming to the wooden steps that climbed the bank. Up, up, monkey and kettle toiled, kettle registering each step with a clank. Bushes beside the steps caught the chain – Woo patiently unwound it. She came at last to a small flat landing. From there a steep clay path ascended to the cottage door. Woo made the discovery here that if the kettle were put on its side it could be rolled. After a brief rest she started to roll it up the steep path, but on a hill the old kettle was other-minded. Dragging Woo with it, from top to bottom it rolled down the entire stair, defeating in seconds Woo's hours of toil and landing just where they started, the kettle spun and settled.

"Ooo!" said the monkey. "Ooo-ooo!"

All concentration was jerked out of her. Picking up a foot she extracted a splinter. She then fell to catching sand-hoppers – a tired but not disheartened monkey, kettle and climb entirely forgotten.

Orgy

Splendid heat roared up my radiators.

"I shall compliment the dealer on this coal," I said.

Before noon stoke-time all the pipes were dead. I went to the basement. The basement had a glass door.

Woo was too absorbed either to see or hear me come. She was walking around carrying in her hands a tin of liquid tar. Every few steps she paused to pour a little tar into any receptacle handy. I saw a black trickle run into my garden hat, which, along with everything else that had been hanging on the basement walls, she had torn down.

The moment my shadow appeared, Woo saw me! Carefully setting the tar can on the floor, she glided into the furnace room. I picked my way among tar puddles. Woo was already seated innocently on her window shelf gazing intently over the tree tops, hands demurely folded in her lap; a loose end of chain dangled from under her chin, another gleam of chain hung down the wall. The ash door of the furnace was flung wide, ashes were raked all over the cement floor. The water-glass egg container yawned on its side, rivers of water-glass ran among the ashes. Egg yolk dripped from the sides of the furnace, from the walls of the room, from door and windows. The coal pile was an omelette. Every bottle in the basement was uncorked, contents had been noted, and either drunk or spilled!

A paper sack containing lime had been emptied into my nail-box, nails stuck out of the lime like little black sticks out of a snow-drift. My geraniums had been transplanted on their heads in eggs and coal. Not a flower-pot was whole.

"Woo! Oh, Woo!"

She neither turned, looked, grinned, nor gibbered. She had had one *good time* and was glad! Stillness brooded over the chaos. Suddenly she caught the broken links of chain, stuffed them in her mouth, gnashed the steel defiantly. Yet I saw that she trembled. I took a split ring and mended the broken chain. She watched. Never had the whites of her eyes looked so uncannily not-white, never her eyelids seemed so uncannily creamily white! Her eyebrows rested far up on her forehead like those of a tired, tired old woman. The little pointed face made me think of an old farm-wife I once knew whose drunken husband so terrified her that she used to run and climb into the tree where her turkeys roosted, peering down at the man through the dusk, her crouched form little bigger than that of her tom turkey.

Woo anticipated a spanking. She did not get it; the spank evaporated from my fingertips! What Woo knew about spanking she had not learned from me. I had seen the hefty black hand of a mother monkey beat her little one; I had seen the big monkeys at the pet shop punish Woo.

She had enjoyed one big blissful orgy! The tantalized curiosity about everything in my basement that lay beyond her chain's length was satisfied at last. Humans had taught Woo to connect the words bad and fun or she would have been delighted with her exploits. In the jungle there is no good and bad, no conscience to tweak.

Poor little Woo! Captivity taught you good – bad.

Woo watched me clean the basement intensely interested. When I looked at her she turned away her eyes. I offered some cracked eggs; her passion for eggs was sated for the moment. The basement decent, the furnace pipes warm, Woo jumped to my shoulder, cooed softly in my ear – luxuriously she stretched her body along the hot pipe and warmed her tummy. Maybe conglomerated soap, blueing, disinfectant, linseed oil, turpentine, worm medicine, mange cure were not sitting quite comfortably there.

I am glad I did not spank Woo, glad she had one huge orgy.

A Boy and
His Dog

◄○►

MARTHA BROOKS

Martha Brooks (b. 1944) was born in Ninette, Manitoba, and now lives in Winnipeg, where she teaches creative writing. Her own novels, plays and short fiction are written from a child's or young adult's perspective. "A Boy and His Dog" depicts what is perhaps the most ancient and enduring of all bonds between humans and animals. Narrated in the language of a teen-age boy ("fourteen going on fifteen"), the story is psychologically credible, both because the loss of a pet is often a child's first experience of death and because a pet, acquired when its owner was an infant, can be the one stable feature for an only child whose parents lead a peripatetic life. On one level "A Boy and His Dog" is a sensitive story of love and loss; on another, arthritic, cancerous Alphonse (a comically aristocratic name for a mongrel) is a metaphor of human aging. The story was published in Paradise Cafe and Other Stories *(1988), a collection aimed at a teenage audience. Brooks has also written A* Hill for Looking *(1982).*

◄ o ►

My dog is old. And he farts a lot. His eyes are constantly runny on account of he's going blind. Sometimes when we go for his walk he falls down. We'll be moving right along, I'll feel an unexpected tug at his leash and bingo! he's over. The first time it happened he cried, sort of whimpered, and looked at his leg, the back one, the one that had betrayed him. I crouched in the tall grass (we take our walks in a sky-filled prairie field near the town-houses where we live) and felt the leg, which was in a spasm. I told him if it didn't work too well to just give up for a while. He seemed to know what I was telling him because he looked at me, whimpered some more, and finally flopped his head back on my leg. That's what kills me about dogs. They figure you're in charge of everything. Like if you pointed your finger, you could make a house fall down. Or if you told them everything's going to be okay, it would be.

After a couple of minutes he stood up and took off again in that business-like, let's-get-the-show-on-the-road manner of his, sniffing, squatting to pee (he doesn't lift his leg anymore) near every bush in sight. Later, I found out he fell over because of arthritis. "Nothing you can do, really," said the vet, patting Alphonse's broad flat head. "He's just getting old, Buddy." She gave me some red pellet-shaped arthritis pills and sent us home.

After that, whenever he fell, he'd look quite cheerful. He'd lick the leg a bit, hang out his tongue, pant, and patiently wait. Just before stumbling to his feet, he'd look up like he was saying thank you – when I hadn't done anything!

I couldn't let him see how bad all this made me feel. He's so smart sometimes you have to put your hands over his ears and spell things so he won't know what you're talking about. Things like cheese, cookie, walk. All his favourites.

Mom said, "He can't last forever. Everybody dies sooner or later. It's the natural course of events. And big dogs don't live as long as little dogs."

Around our house, nobody put their hands over my ears.

Alphonse was a present for my first birthday. Dad brought him home, just a scruffy little brown pup someone was giving away. No special breed. I still have a snapshot of him and me at the party. I was this goopy-looking blond kid in blue corduroy overalls and a Donald Duck T-shirt. Alphonse was all over me in the way of puppies. I'd been startled by Dad's flash and also by Alphonse, who'd chosen that exact moment to paw me down and slurp strawberry ice cream off my face and hands. Dad says I didn't cry or anything! Just lay bug-eyed on the shag rug with Alphonse wiggling and slopping all over me. We got on like a house on fire after that.

Which is why it's so unfair that I'm fourteen going on fifteen and he's thirteen going on ninety-four.

I guess I thought we'd just go on forever with Alphonse being my dog. Listening when I tell him stuff. When he goes, who am I going to tell my secrets to? I tell him things I wouldn't even tell Herb Malken, who is my best friend now that we've been in this city a year. My dad's always getting transferred. He's in the army. When I grow up that's one thing I'm not going to be. In the army. I won't make my kids move every three years and leave all their friends behind. Which is one thing I *am* going to do: have more than one kid when I get married.

There's a big myth that only children are selfish and self-centred. I can say from personal experience that only children are more likely to feel guilty and be too eager to please. It's terrible when you are one kid having to be everything to two parents.

Which is why Alphonse is more than just a dog, you see. Mom even sometimes calls him "Baby." Like he's my brother. Which it sometimes feels like.

Last week he had bad gas. I always sleep with the window open. Even so, it got pretty awful in my bedroom.

Alphonse doesn't make much sound when he farts. Just a little "phhhht" like a balloon with a slow leak and there's no living with him. I swear when he gets like that it would be dangerous to light a match.

I sent him out. He went obligingly. He's always been a polite dog. I listened, first to his toenails clicking over the hardwood floors, then to the scratching of his dry bristly fur as he slumped against the other side of the bedroom door. When you can't be in the same room with someone who's shared your dreams for thirteen years, it's hard to get properly relaxed. It isn't the same when they aren't near you, breathing the same air.

For the next few days he lay around more than usual. I thought perhaps he was just overtired (even though I hadn't been able to stand it and had begun to let him back into my room, farts and all). By Sunday, Mom cocked her head at him and said to Dad and me, "I don't like the way Alphonse looks. Better take him back to the vet, Buddy."

Mom works at the army base too. It's late when she and Dad get home and by that time the vet is closed for the day. So I always take Alphonse right after school. It isn't far – three blocks past the field.

Monday was the kind of fall day that makes you breathe more deeply – the field all burning colours, far-off bushes little flames of magenta and orange, dry wavy grass a pale yellow, and the big sky that kind of deep fire blue you see only once a year, in October. Alphonse didn't fall down once. Eyes half closed, he walked slowly, sniffing the air to take in messages.

A young ginger-coloured cat slithered under a wooden fence and into the field. It saw Alphonse and suddenly crouched low, eyes dark, motionless. For a minute there I didn't think he would notice it. Then his ears went up and his head shot forward. Next thing, he was hauling me along at the end of his leash, barking himself into a frenzy. The cat parted the grass like wildfire and, reaching the fence, dug its body gracelessly under at a spot where there seemed hardly an inch between wood and solid earth.

Alphonse has that effect on cats. They must think he's death on wheels the way they scatter to get out of his way. He stared proudly in the direction of the fence; his nose hadn't failed him. He walked on, a little more vigour in his step, his tongue lolling out, his ears nice and perky.

We reached the edge of the field where we usually turn around on our walks. This time, of course, we didn't. He lost some of his bounce and trailed slightly behind. I looked back. He lowered his head. "She's not going to do anything to you, you crazy dog," I told him. "She's going to shake her head again, and tell us to go home." He kept pace with me after that. Like I said, dogs believe everything you tell them.

The vet is the kind of person whose job runs her life. One minute she's smiling over a recovering patient, or one who's come in just for shots; the next, she's blowing her nose like the place is a funeral parlor. It must be murder to become so involved with your patients. She always looks as if she needs some place to hole up for a good sleep. And her legs are magnets for strays who are forever up for adoption.

At the clinic, I sat down with Alphonse resignedly backed up between my knees. To my astonishment, a resident cat sauntered over and actually rubbed against him. Alphonse sniffed its head and then ignored it (he only likes cats who run). He watched the door to the examining room and trembled. I wondered if his eyesight was improving. With one hand I held his leash; the other I bit away at because of hangnails.

When the vet, smiling, summoned us, I got to my feet and Alphonse reluctantly pattered after me. Inside the examining room he pressed against the door, willing it to open. I picked him up and lugged him over to the table.

"He's lost weight," said the vet, stroking, prodding gently.

"He was too fat," I said, patting his stomach.

She laughed, continuing her way down his body. "Has he been on a diet?"

"No. I guess older dogs don't eat as much – like older people."

She looked at his rectum. "How long has this been here?" she said softly, more to herself than to me.

"This what?" I looked.

"It's quite a small lump," she said, pressing it hard.

Alphonse stood politely on the table, shaking and puffing.

"Sometimes," she said, with a reassuring smile, "older dogs get these lumps and they usually aren't anything to worry about, Buddy."

Usually? What did she mean, *usually?* My heart began to race.

"Older neutered dogs," she continued, in the same even tone, "very often get benign lumps in the anal region. But we'd better check this out, anyway . . ."

My dog has cancer. What do I tell him now? What am I going to do? Mom and Dad have left it up to me. The vet, with strained sad eyes, says the little lump is just a symptom of what's going on inside. Why didn't I notice that he was so short of breath? That he was peeing more than usual? That he didn't eat much? That his bowels weren't working? She tells me that when dogs are old all of these things become a problem, it's the usual progress of aging. Except not in Alphonse's case. But how would I know that? I shouldn't blame myself. She says there was nothing I could have done to stop it, anyway.

So what do I tell him? Is he in pain? I couldn't stand it if he were in pain. Tonight Mom wanted to give me a sleeping pill. I refused it. Alphonse is here with me on my bed. He's going to sleep with me one last time. I'll hold him and tell him about me and what I plan to do with my life. I'll have to lie a little, fill in a few places, because I'm not *exactly* sure. But he has a right to know what he'll be missing. I'll have a good life, I know it, just like he's had. I'm going to tell him about it now, whisper it in his ear, and I won't leave out a single detail.

The Black Stallion
and the Red Mare

◄○►

GLADYS FRANCIS LEWIS

*Gladys Francis Lewis (1900-1985) is a native of Ontario who lived
for many years in Saskatoon, receiving a degree in English from the
University of Saskatchewan. Her stories were at one time well
known, for they were used in the Copp Clark school readers and
also appeared in popular journals, including* Reader's Digest. *"The
Black Stallion and the Red Mare" describes one of the wild herds
that were common in the wilderness areas and grazing lands of
Western Canada. Though the horses were, for many, romantic
symbols of freedom, ranchers and farmers regarded them as
expendable predators. The great black stallion, "the hero or the
villain of a hundred tales," belongs with Chief Buffalo Child Long
Lance's legendary Ghost Horse that haunted the upper Columbia*

river plateau, with the Steel-grey Killer that travelled the Alberta plains, with the Racing White Stallion who combined several remarkable animals in one persona – all of them superior steeds to whom legends accrued. Lewis provides an ending that reconciles Donald's divided loyalties.

Herds of wild horses, descendants of stock which migrating farmers left behind in the Thirties, still roam the Canadian prairies. They are admired by breeders who prize their glossy coats, muscular bodies and ability to outrun domestic animals. Traditionalists nostalgically associate them with the horses that served native peoples, explorers, settlers and cowboys, making them part of the "western heritage." However, in recent years the herds have provoked confrontations between animal rights activists and traditionalists, on the one hand, and environmentalists, on the other. The latter point out that the horses' domination of grasslands forces out antelope and deer, and threatens with extinction fragile plant forms. In 1994, after a civilian committee had recommended that a one thousand strong herd on the Canadian Forces Base at Suffield be completely removed, it was decided that rather than being slaughtered, the healthy animals should be sold individually to ranchers, Indian bands and anyone else able to provide a home.

◄○►

At first Donald lay still. Scarcely a muscle moved. The boulders and the low shrubs screened him from view. Excitement held him motionless. His hands gripped the short grass and his toes dug into the dry earth. Cautiously he raised himself on his elbows and gazed at the scene below him.

There, in his father's unfenced hay flats, was the outlaw band of wild horses. They were grazing quietly on the rich grass. Some drank from the small hillside stream. Donald tried to count them, but they suddenly began moving about and he could not get beyond twenty. He thought there might be two hundred.

Donald knew a good deal about that band of horses, but he had never had the good luck to see them. They were known over many hundreds of square miles. They had roamed at will over the grain fields and they had led away many a domestic horse to the wild life. Once in that band, a horse was lost to the farm.

There in the flats was the great black stallion, the hero or the villain of a hundred tales. Over the far-flung prairie and grass lands there was scarcely a boy who had not dreamed of wild rides, with the great body of the stallion beneath him, bearing him clean through the air with the sharp speed of lightning.

There was the stallion now, moving among the horses with the sureness and ease of a master. As he moved about, teasingly kicking here and nipping there, a restlessness, as of a danger sensed, stirred through the band. The stallion cut to the outside of the group. At a full gallop he snaked around the wide circle, roughly bunching the mares and colts into the smaller circle of an invisible corral.

He was a magnificent creature, huge and proudly built. Donald saw the gloss of the black coat and the great curving muscles of the strong legs, the massive hoofs, the powerful arch of the neck, the proud crest of the head. Donald imagined he could see the flash of black, intelligent eyes. Surely a nobler creature never roamed the plains!

Off-wind from the herd, a red mare came out from the fold of the low hills opposite. She stood motionless a moment, her graceful head held high. Then she nickered. The black stallion drew up short in his herding, nickered eagerly, then bolted off in the direction of the mare. She stood waiting until he had almost reached her; then they galloped back to the herd together.

The shadows crept across the hay flats and the evening stillness settled down. A bird sang sleepily on one note. Donald suddenly became aware of the monotonous song, and stirred from his intent watching. He must tell his father and help send news around the countryside. He was still intensely excited as he crept back from the brow of the hill and hurried home. All the time his mind was busy and his heart was bursting.

Donald knew that three hundred years ago the Spaniards had brought horses to Mexico. Descendants of these horses had wandered into the Great Plains. These horses he now was watching were of that Spanish strain. Thousands of them roamed the cattle lands north to the American boundary. This band now grazed wild over these park lands here in Canada – four hundred and fifty miles north of the boundary.

His father and the farmers for many miles around had determined to round up the horses and make an end of the roving band. As a farmer's son, Donald knew that this was necessary and right. But a certain respect for the band and the fierce loyalty that he felt toward all wild, free creatures made him wish in his heart that they might never be caught, never be broken and tamed. He, who was so full of sympathy for the horses, must be traitor to them!

There had been conflicts in his heart before, but never had there been such a warring of two strong loyalties. He saw himself for the first time as a person of importance because he, Donald Turner, had the power to affect the lives of others. This power, because it could help or harm others, he knew he must use wisely.

When he stood before his father half an hour later, he did not blurt out his news. It was too important for that. But his voice and his eyes were tense with excitement. "That band of wild horses is in the hay hollow west of the homestead quarter," he said. "There must be close to two hundred."

His father was aware of the boy's deep excitement. At Donald's first words he stopped his milking, his hands resting on the rim of the pail as he looked up.

"Good lad, Donald!" he said, quietly enough. "Get your supper and we'll ride to Smith's and Duncan's to start the word around. Tell Mother to pack lunches for tomorrow. We'll start at sunup." He turned to his milking again.

The other men were in the yard shortly after daylight.

Donald afterward wondered how long it would have taken ranch hands to round up the band of horses. These farmers knew horses, but not how to round up large numbers of them as the men of the ranch country knew so well. The farmers learned a good deal in the next two weeks.

Twenty men started out after the band as it thundered out of the hay flats, through the hills and over the country. The dust rose in clouds as their pounding hoofs dug the dry earth. The herd sped before the pursuers with the effortless speed of the wind. The black stallion led or drove his band, and kept them well together. That first day only the young colts were taken.

At sunset the riders unsaddled and staked their horses by a poplar thicket, ate their stale lunches and lay down to sleep under the stars. Their horses cropped the short grass and drank from the stream. Some slept standing, others lay down.

At dawn the herd was spied moving westward. With the coming of night, they, too, had rested. For a mile or more they now sped along the rim of a knoll, swift as broncos pulled in off the range after a winter out. The black stallion was a hundred feet ahead, running with a tireless, easy swing, his mane and tail streaming and his body stretched level as it cut through the morning mists. Close at his side, but half a length behind him, ran the red mare. The band streamed after.

After the first day's chase and the night under the stars, Donald had ridden back home. Not that he had wanted to go back. He would have given everything that he owned to have gone on with the men. But there were horses and cattle and chores to attend to at home, and there was school.

The roundup continued. Each day saw the capture of more and more horses. As the men doubled back on their course, they began to see that the wild horses traveled in a great circle, coming back again and again over the same ground, stopping at the same watering holes and feeding in the same rich grass flats. Once this course became clear, fresh riders and mounts in relays were posted along the way, while others drove on from behind. The wild band had still to press on with little chance for rest and feeding. The strain of the pursuit took away their desire for food, but they had a burning thirst and the black stallion would never let them drink their fill before he drove them on. Fatigue grew on them.

As the roundup continued, the whole countryside stirred with excitement. At every town where there was a grain elevator along the railroad, people repeated the latest news of the chase. On the farms the hay went unmown or unraked, and the plows rested still in the last furrow of the summer fallow. At school the children played roundup at recess. Donald, at his desk, saw the printed pages of his books, but his mind was miles away running with the now almost exhausted wild horses.

Near the end of the second week of the chase, Donald's father rode into the yard. Donald dropped the wood he was carrying to the house and ran to meet his father.

"Dad, they haven't got the black stallion and the red mare, have they?" Donald could scarcely wait for his father's slow reply.

"No, Donald, lad," he said. "Though those two are the only horses still free. They're back in the flats. We'll get them tomorrow."

Donald felt both relief and fear.

In the yellow lamplight of the supper table his father told of the long days of riding, of the farms where he had eaten and rested, and of the adventures of each day.

"That was a gallant band, lad!" he said. "Never shall we see their equal! Those two that are left are a pair of great horses. Most wild horses show a weakening in the strain and grow up with little wind or muscle. But these two are sound of wind and their muscles are like steel. Besides that, they have intelligence. They would have been taken long ago but for that."

No one spoke. Donald felt that his father was on his side, the side of the horses. After a long pause, Mr. Turner continued.

"With his brains and his strength, that stallion could have got away in the very beginning. He could have got away a dozen times and would now be free south of the border. But that was his band. He stayed by them, and he tried to get them to safety. This week, when his band had been rounded up, he stuck by that red mare. She is swift but she can't match his speed. It's curious the way they keep together. He stops and nickers. She nickers in reply and comes close to him, her nose touching his flank. They stand a moment. Then they are away again, she running beside him but not quite neck to neck. Day after day it is the same. They are no ordinary horseflesh, those two, lad!"

There was a lump in Donald's throat. He knew what his father meant. Those horses seemed to stand for something bigger and greater than himself. There were other things that made him feel the same – the first full-throated song of the meadow lark in the spring; ripe golden fields of wheat with the breeze rippling it in waves; the sun setting over the rim of the world in a blaze of rose and gold; the sun rising again in the quiet east; the smile in the blue depths of his mother's eyes; the still whiteness of the snow-bound plains; the story of Columbus dauntlessly sailing off into unknown seas.

These things were part of a hidden, exciting world. The boy belonged to these things in some strange way. He caught only glimpses of that hidden world, but those glimpses were tantalizing. Something deep within him leaped up in joy.

That night Donald dreamed of horses nickering to him but, when he tried to find them, they were no longer there. Then he dreamed that he was riding the great, black stallion, riding over a far-flung range, riding along a hilltop road with the world spread below him on every side. He felt the powerful body of the horse beneath him. He felt the smooth curves of the mighty muscles. Horse and rider seemed as one.

A cold dawn shattered his glorious dream ride. With his father he joined the other horsemen. From the crest of the slope from which Donald had first seen them, the pair of horses was sighted. They were dark moving shadows in the gray mists of the morning.

They had just finished drinking deep from the stream. Not for two weeks had the men seen the horses drink like that. Thirsty as they were, they had taken but one drink at each water hole. This last morning they were jaded and spent; they had thrown caution to the winds.

At the first suspicion of close danger, they stood still, heads and tails erect. Then they dashed toward the protecting hills. There the way forked.

It was then Donald saw happen the strange thing his father had described. At the fork the stallion halted and nickered. The mare answered and came close. She touched his flank with her head. Then they bounded off and disappeared in the path that led north-west to the rougher country where the chase had not led before.

Along the way the horses had been expected to take, grain-fed horses had been stationed. These had now to move over north-west. But the men were in no hurry today. They were sure of the take before nightfall. The sun was low in the west when two riders spurred their mounts for the close in. The stallion and the mare were not a hundred yards ahead. They were dead spent. Their glossy coats were flecked with dark foam. Fatigue showed in every line of their bodies. Their gallant spirits no longer could drive their spent bodies. The stallion called to the mare. He heard her answer behind him. He slowed down, turning wildly in every direction. She came up to him, her head drooped on his flank and rested there. In a last wild defiance, the stallion tossed

his magnificent head and drew strength for a last mighty effort. Too late!

The smooth coils of a rope tightened around his feet. He was down, down and helpless. He saw the mare fall as the rope slipped over her body and drew tight around her legs. It maddened him. He struggled wildly to be free. The taut rope held. The stallion was conquered. In that last struggle something went out of him. Broken was his body and broken was his spirit. Never again would he roam the plains, proud and free, the monarch of his herd.

Donald saw it all. He felt it all. His hands gripped the pommel of the saddle and his knees pressed hard against his pony's sides. Tears blinded his eyes and from his throat came the sound of a single sob. It was as if he himself were being broken and tied.

The sun dipped below the rim of the plains. The day was gone; the chase was ended. The men stood about smoking and talking in groups of two's and three's, examining the two roped horses. Donald's father knelt close to the mare, watching her intently. Donald watched him. His father remained quiet for a moment, one knee still resting on the ground, in his hand his unsmoked pipe. Donald waited for his father to speak. At last the words came.

"Boys," he said, without looking up, and with measured words, "do you know, this mare is blind – stone blind!"

A week later, Donald and his father stood watching those two horses in the Turner corral. They were not the same spirited creatures, but they were still magnificent horses.

"I figured," his father said, turning to the boy, "that they had won the right to stay together. I've brought them home for you, Donald. They are yours, lad. I know you will be good to them."

Jeannot the Crow

◄○►

GABRIELLE ROY

Gabrielle Roy (1909-1983) was born in St. Boniface, Manitoba. She taught for several years in Manitoba before settling in Quebec. Her literary career began in 1937 with stories and articles published by La Liberté *in St. Boniface. Subsequently her novels and essays won Governor-General's Literary awards and the Prix Fémina (France). A persistent theme is the communion between a lonely individual and the world of nature.* Cet été qui chantait *(1972), published in English as* Enchanted Summer *(1976), is a collection of nature sketches set in rural Quebec. The landscape consists of a village surrounded by farms, a wooded mountain, a tidal river, a tranquil railroad, its embankment a profusion of wildflowers – primroses, columbines, bluebells. Here "the lady from the summer cottage" observes and* records the activities of killdeer, crows, swallows, cedar waxwings, robins, hummingbirds, of a frog, a horse, a dog, of cats and cows – all of them friends who enliven our "tedious earthly life."

The inspiration for these impressionistic essays, according to an autobiographical source, La détresse et l'enchantement, was a letter from her cloistered sister Dédette celebrating humble beauties – "le feu des lucioles, le chant de la vague, celui des feuillages, le cri d'un oiseau traversant l'espace." In such simple images can be felt "un peu de la pulsation du grand songe de Dieu."

For "Jeannot the Crow" (translated by Joyce Marshall), Roy's painterly eye condenses the landscape of Charlevoix Country into a single magnificent wild red cherry tree which, pruned, fertilized and watered, has become a lyre, a vase overflowing with flowers, a young woman shaking her outspread hair and, on windy days, a swing for a friendly crow. Jeannot is differentiated from his flock and given a personality, not only by the attribute of a name but also by the author's use of verbs that normally designate the activities of people – pilfer, dream, contemplate, board the sailing ship. This story is a celebration of simple joys; it is also a testimony to life's brevity, for in these few pages Roy replicates the mood described in Fragiles lumières de la terre (The Fragile Lights of Earth [1978]):

> At certain times, when our heart is free to welcome it, it is the spell of the universe: the long waves rolling immutably toward the sands of the shore; the free creatures of every species; the trees, and the wind's music in the treetops; summer, winter, the charm of the seasons; in the place that is home, so manifestly made for us that all our lives we suffer secretly at the notion that we will one day be torn from it.

Additional works on a similar theme include La petite poule d'eau (Where Nests the Water Hen) *(1950);* La Montagne secrète (The Hidden Mountain) *(1961);* La Rivière sans repos (Windflower) *(1970) and* Ces enfants de ma vie (Children of My Heart) *(1977).*

◄o►

I

Nothing in this world is more difficult than to distinguish one crow from another. If I was finally able to recognize Jeannot, this was because he came without fail on days when the wind sang from the southwest, to perch in the delicate tip of my wild red cherry tree and let himself be rocked for a long time, the tree in this summer wind being simply a swing in the sky.

None of our other trees can be compared to this wild red cherry. We began to shape it when it was still a sapling, pruning here, straightening there, rectifying this; and just as with human beings when you apply yourself to them in time and gently, we obtained astonishing results. The tree is so striking now that it is always compared to something other than a tree. In repose, with the wind playing on it with muted strings, it is a lyre. Viewed from below and a slight distance, it looks like a vase overflowing with flowers on a shelf above the ocean. When the wild wind flings its leaves forward as if over a face, it suggests a young woman shaking and shaking her outspread hair with joyful movements of the head.

However, it is in the southwest wind with Jeannot at its tip that our wild red cherry tree is most graceful.

Many of our friends exclaim when they visit us for the first time, "What a beautiful tree! Where did it come from? From what country?"

At first we used to reply that it was an ordinary little tree of a sort that grows all along the cliff, native to these parts, nothing more. That we'd only had to prune it a trifle, encourage it, give it water and fertilizer. Now we feel compassion for the bewilderment these simple remarks always awaken on people's faces, as if they can't bear the idea that they might do as much. Perhaps it's having to do as much that appals them. Now when our guests exclaim, "What a tree! You must have had it brought from far away," we say nothing to make them think otherwise. And in one sense it's true that our wild red cherry tree comes from far away.

As you might expect, the birds are very much attached to it. With most of them, it must be admitted, from self-interest. A few years ago I noticed that cedar waxwings, beguiling birds with crew cuts, arrived almost every day in July, seven or eight of them together, to perch here and there in the tree. After a while I realized that they had come to see whether the little fruit, which were just beginning to take colour, would soon be good to eat. At last one day they were ready and in an instant the tree was stripped. For the rest of that summer I never saw another cedar waxwing.

But the following summer they were outwitted. Six big blue jays in company discovered that there were some of these exquisite fruit in our yard. Through the red clusters one morning I glimpsed their brilliant uniforms of cobalt blue. The shriek of a soul in agony rose a short distance away where a seventh jay stood sentinel, and nothing is less appropriate to these splendid uhlans than this truly terrible shriek. Seated in the tree, the six jays feasted. The berries, however, weren't quite ripe. The cedar waxwings had dropped by the previous day to taste them and had decided to give them one more day. Much good it did them. When they returned on the morrow, the cupboard was bare.

But the next summer the blue jays were forestalled in turn. Evening grosbeaks, seemingly less finicky than the greedy jays, arrived early one July morning and cleaned the cherry tree of its small fruit while they were still green. Perhaps it gave them indigestion. Served them right.

But let me come at last to my subject, for if I've mentioned these successive raids, it was to show the difference between Jeannot and other birds. He at least came to the tree neither to eat nor even to sleep but only, as far as I could tell, from affection.

I daresay he pilfered elsewhere. A bit to the right, a bit to the left, so that it was not too apparent in any one garden: for instance, a leaf of red lettuce from Lucienne, my third neighbour – and how could a crow fail to appreciate the tasty lettuce that we were all constantly begging for ourselves?; perhaps a few sweet juicy cherries from Berthe; and here and there, from people who still had the heart to grow them, that delicacy of all crows, the seeds of those giant sunflowers that used to bloom everywhere of old. But from me Jeannot took nothing.

Besides, he came only when the rocking wind blew, bowing our little tree endlessly against the background of sea. Days without wind and without music, "dead" days when I myself grow lonely – perhaps for eternity – there was no sign of Jeannot. But as soon as the song of the rustling leaves resumed, I could be sure I'd see my crow again. Shortly afterwards, in fact, I would discern in the intensely blue sky an approaching speck of black.

Sometimes he'd have trouble navigating so as to land precisely in the middle of the cherry tree. He'd be obliged to repeat his approach again and again, carried each time into the distance. He'd then glide on motionless wings, and to recover his speed and momentum, he'd turn at the base of the mountain where the air is always calm. At last he would manage to make a perfect landing on his little perch. This was a tiny fork formed by two supple twigs high in the tree. Once settled and sure of his equilibrium, Jeannot would relax and let himself be carried fearlessly from one side of the horizon to the other.

In this way, by certain infallible signs, I learned a few years ago to recognize a friendly crow.

Jeannot never slept in the tree. With the field glasses I would see his eyes glinting in his black shiny face. Nor did he give any of those caws that grate so on the nerves. He was quite silent. He seemed to be there only to dream while contemplating the mountains, the whitecaps on the river and, far in the distance, the line of the south shore, always somewhat hazy on warm days. Like a small black lookout in the crow's-nest of a ship, he swung back and forth in the sky.

By other characteristics too – a way of holding his head to one side, a stiffness in his right wing as if it had once been slightly injured – I became better and better able to recognize my gentle crow. I could finally follow most of the activities and movements of his life.

First of all, where he spent the night. In a tree but this as different from our little wild red cherry as day is from night. A tall melancholy tree, shaggy, dead on one side and with numerous long branches, some dry, others leafy, a very old maple with room, storey upon storey, for the whole tribe to settle at nightfall, in families. At the end of a wild field, on a desolate plateau in a remote spot and with sombre woods in the background, it had been known for as long as anyone remembered as the Tree of Crows. When they gathered there at dusk, the tree, already dark by nature, looked truly fearsome with those little pitch-black shapes pressed against one another along all the branches, even the skeletal ones. What did it look like then? Well, what else but a scarecrow made of crows?

To those of the species who didn't lack humour or a comic sense, it was perhaps amusing to inhabit a tree that seemed designed to scare them away.

At sunrise, however, nothing was gayer for a brief moment than that ancient tree with all its tenants in a great commotion of departure, giving voice to resounding caws. The new light awoke iridescences in the lustrous plumage that the vainest among them were still polishing with their beaks. Then they rose together into the sky and the old maple fell back into its mournful solitude.

The crows then broke ranks. Some, the more sociable, proceeded to the charming town of Baie-Saint-Paul where there were well-tended gardens to pillage. Others chose the uninhabited wild region of the abandoned pool of Monsieur Toong, the bullfrog. Still others remained in Petite-Rivière-Saint-François and spent their days flying round the mountain and along the shore of the river.

My Jeannot was rather solitary; by day he seldom rejoined his kin. He was even less inclined to fraternize with the gulls gathered in compact groups on the rocks uncovered by the receding tide. A few crows risked it, however, and there was no more curious sight in the empty immensity of the river than this close companionship on the crests of breakers of black birds and white birds. When I examined them with field glasses, however, I never caught them conversing with one another. They were together, it's true, but apparently without any sort of communication. And from afar, thus assembled and yet not acquainted, they resembled human beings.

What did Jeannot do all day? Unquestionably, if the wind was favourable, not much else but rock in the tree. He also pilfered a bit from the gardens to right and left. As his territory was so restricted, he finally drew attention to himself and in the course of the summer I began to hear threatening remarks directed at Jeannot.

"That dratted crow!" grumbled Monsieur Simon, my neighbour. "I'll settle his hash!"

As excuse for Monsieur Simon and several other enemies of the crows, I should mention the trouble they'd had that year rescuing their fruit and vegetables from caterpillars, slugs and potato bugs. And now it looked as if the crows would snatch what remained from under their noses. Yet it seemed unjust to me that all the blame should fall on the head of poor Jeannot, who was perhaps less prompt than other crows to make off when Monsieur Simon approached, sweeping the air with his arms and shouting, "Dratted crow! Dratted crow!"

Besides, how could Monsieur Simon imagine that he was always dealing with the same crow, since he had never learned to distinguish one from another with the eyes of affection?

However, while believing that he was speaking each day to the same crow, Monsieur Simon managed to offend a good many birds – from the most scatterbrained to the oldest and most dignified. The tribe finally banded together to harass this man of such little perspicacity. From then on there was always one looting his garden while another drew his attention elsewhere.

He took to lying in ambush in his lilac hedge, loaded rifle in hand. One afternoon I thought I heard through the rustling of the leaves the sound of a shot from the garden next door. I was very anxious for a few minutes.

But soon, a black speck in the radiant immensity, Jeannot appeared. He came, moreover, from the opposite direction to the dangerous garden. For that day at least he had not joined in the foray against Monsieur Simon.

He sank to his perch as gently as a flower drops from its stem. He remained for a good twenty minutes that day, I believe, huddled in his little niche, journeying across the sky.

II

The next month was one of the most pleasant I can remember. The southwest wind filled the air almost continually with the roaring of a river that must have flowed for days and days. All living creatures were lulled by this strange and mysterious river, Jeannot in the cherry tree, I in my wooden swing, Aimé's cows motionless at my fence, delivered for one more day from gnats and horseflies. From moment to moment, borne on the moving air as if on a high and sonorous wave, sounded the melodious tinkle of the bell the Rover set in motion each time she craned her neck to reach over the hedge for a cool leaf.

This blessed wind I imagine as having been born in a distant happy country where beings never hunt one another but live quietly side by side. Furthermore, I noticed that it was only on such days that the black birds on the exposed rocks far away in the murmuring water joined with the white birds.

My Jeannot arrived almost every day now at a regular hour. He came to rest between two thefts. Mere trifles: a leaf of Lucienne's fine lettuce, a strawberry at Berthe's and, more serious, three pecks from a tomato that might never heal.

"That cursed black devil!" I thought I heard in the distance.

Completely safe with me, wings pressed to his body and head tucked in, Jeannot travelled through the sky.

There were calm periods. Then the wind stilled and, the music of the foliage abruptly silent, we were back feet first in what is called "reality," and it seemed insufficient, confining, intolerable. But soon the atmosphere would resound again with the stereophonic music of those summer days in the country.

Truly it is a complex music and requires the participation of many players. To my left, the house of my closest neighbour is enclosed by a group of old willow trees with heavy branches. It is here the wind attacks. As it forces a passage through the low and often deformed branches, it acquires that deep voice of a powerful river. You can hear the abundant water, at once free and confined, discharging no one knows where. This is the bass that supports the voices of the more subtle instruments. Suddenly the wind has crossed the road and given the signal to my pines. Nothing is silkier than their masses of fine needles and here the wind stirs eddy after eddy. In these eddies you can hear the most curious sound ever to come from a tree; it's like the passing of a little country train, very far in the distance, perhaps only in memory. Next the music is communicated to my wood of aspens and silver birches, about thirty of them together on the edge of a ravine. In this grove of young trees the wind suggests the trickling of a cool brook. Trickle, trickle, a young brook trickles steadily in my wood of birch and aspen.

Finally the instruments combine to take up the theme of triumphant summer. All is peace on such days, even though every form of plant life shakes, bows and dances about like a musician under the baton of an orchestra leader, even the grasses at the foot of the trees gone mad, running and running in place, without ever finding time to straighten up. The river in the misshapen willows, the faraway train among the pines, the swift brook on the edge of the ravine, all speak of a mysterious and secret accord.

On these days of full-throated music, my wild red cherry tree, a quivering silhouette against the backdrop of the river, can scarcely make its muted song be heard.

So without contributing much to the symphony of the world, it sways at least to its own rhythm, all sails unfurled. With the black bird aboard and me in my garden chair, we spent many hours travelling together on the same wave of time.

III

But alas, Jeannot was growing old. He was becoming less prompt at extracting himself from scrapes. More than once I had heard a bullet whistle perilously close to him when he stopped off in passing to have a bite at Monsieur Simon's. I had told him to be careful, that misfortune would come from that side. But he was never one to take advice willingly from humans. Or from his own tribe either. He was a loner.

I was waiting for him one day in my place in the garden. The air stirred the leaves, the pine needles, the grasses. It was a day fashioned in every respect to delight Jeannot. Then through the vocal ensemble that at times so closely imitates the wind high in the sky, I thought I heard the dull sound of a shot. How anxious I felt as I scanned the unbroken blue of the sky. But then, what a relief, the familiar little shape appeared. I was about to laugh once more at the fruitless efforts of Monsieur Simon when – misfortune – the bird plunged towards the ground like a plane in distress. Oh little friend, I thought, at least don't fall on the road where car after car will run over your crushed body.

Jeannot exerted a surprising effort. Steadying himself more or less, he reached a current of air that carried him almost to my yard. Just before he managed it, however, he almost fell again, climbed clumsily, dragged himself, you might say, on his wings to a point just over the cherry tree. At that moment the air ceased almost all movement, as if to aid the wounded bird. His perch received him. Once again he dug in his claws. The gentle wind resumed and wafted him through the sky.

Then the little form at the heart of the tree collapsed, suddenly soft. Jeannot's attire of such beautiful black caught fire as a ray of sun pierced the foliage, making it shine between the branches like a polished coal.

At once the gulls announced high in the sky that Jeannot was dead. Though he had never stood with them in strange companionship on the exposed rocks when the tide rose or fell, nevertheless they were the first to mourn him.

"Jeannot is dead! Jeannot is dead!"

Thus the news reached a huge detachment of crows just returning from Baie-Saint-Paul. As one they continued their flight straight to Monsieur Simon's, crying, "He's the culprit! He's the one!"

Never have I seen so many birds rise up in so little time and from all sides at once. They came from the high fields between the village and the mountain ridge. They came from the more distant hollows behind that first ridge. They came from the fields below. And all converged upon Monsieur Simon's garden.

The poor man must have believed that the birds had gone mad and his last hour was at hand. Beating at the air with his hands, he ran here and there, shouting till he was breathless, "Go away! Go away!"

Far from going away, the birds inscribed great circles in the air, descending lower and lower to brush against Monsieur Simon. And they shouted at him in turn, "Caw caw! Shame and pity! To have killed Jeannot for a tomato!"

Finally they left a place now forever detestable in their sight. They flew to my house and circled round the small black shape in the branches, chanting the funeral service of Jeannot. At last the wind swept him to the ground. I asked Aimé to come then and together we dug a grave at the foot of the wild red cherry tree. Here Jeannot reposes.

And since that day the crows have never failed to call to me as they pass, "Caw, caw, caw!"

Christmas Goose

◄O►

BARBARA GRANTMYRE

Barbara Grantmyre (1903-1977) was born in England but came as a child to Nova Scotia, where she spent the rest of her life. Her work appeared on radio and television, in magazines like Cosmopolitan *and in short story collections. The source of "Christmas Goose" was a CBC radio programme,* Stories with John Drainie, *which aired from 1:45 to 2:00 P.M. on weekdays. Running from 1959 until 1967, it attracted 10,000 submissions, all under 1,800 words in length so that they could be read in ten minutes. Though, according to Drainie's daughter Bronwyn, the quality was unremarkable, the well-known Canadian actor transformed the "straw, if not into gold, at least into attractive silver plate." Thirty-five of them were published under the programme title,* Stories with John Drainie *(Toronto: Ryerson Press, 1963).*

"Christmas Goose" is patterned like a traditional folk-tale. A wild bird which hunters have injured is saved by children and becomes a "helpful animal" in their home. But she inspires hatred in the father, who determines to get rid of her. In folk-tale fashion, "all's well that ends well." In spite of the archetypes, "Christmas Goose" is a realistic vignette of a kind of rural poverty common in Canada fifty years ago, the time in which the story is set. Barbara Grantmyre's other work includes Lunar Rogue *(1963),* The River That Missed the Boat *(1975) and a short story collection,* A Rose for Minnie Mullet *(1964).*

◄o►

The first thing Sawkey noticed when he came home that night in late November was the feathered head snaking up from the clothes basket back of the stove. It gave him quite a turn.

"What's going on?"

"A wild goose, Pa. Lem and the twins found it on Berrigan bog."

"It's got a hurted wing."

"We thought it was dead."

"Poor thing! It's remarkable tame, Sawkey. Lem bandaged it with no trouble. He ought to be a veterny, that boy."

"Not hurt bad, Pa. Just a scrape. Some of the long feathers are busted so it can't fly. I guess they'll grow in."

"Stand back, everybody, while I look at the creature." Sawkey pushed two or three youngsters aside and went to the basket.

"Sssst!" Two bright eyes caught the lamplight and tried to stare him down.

Lem had bandaged the injured wing and put straw in the basket for a bed. The goose, black-headed with two white cheek patches, sign of the true Canada goose and not the lesser brant, seemed comfortable enough, though a spark of animosity showed as Sawkey peered down.

Sawkey Mullet was a kind man. He wouldn't kick a dog or prod an ox with a pitchfork, so for a moment he was bewildered at the sudden strong dislike he felt for the hapless bird. Then it came to him.

"Great swith! This goose is the spittin' image of Malvola Piper," he exclaimed.

"Malvola Piper?" repeated Minnie. "One of the back-river Pipers?"

"Nah! Malvola hailed from Cumberland County . . . or maybe Yarmouth. She was a mean, spiteful, old maid school teacher who'd rather lick you than learn you. I had her in fifth grade. That term I got more trimmings for less cause than all the rest of my schooldays. Gar! I hated Malvola."

"Malvola's a pretty name, though," put in Lem. "Let's call the goose Malvola."

"Better call her Dinner, boy. She'll make a mighty tasty feed." Sawkey's words caused a wail of dismay. Even Minnie looked distressed.

"We can't eat the poor thing. She's Lem's, and so kind it's amazing."

"She'll hurt somebody. You can't trust a wild creature. Suppose she attacked the baby?"

To prove him wrong, the baby, who had been crawling by the woodbox, hoisted himself to the basket and reached for the bird. The bird with a soft honk arched its neck gently and let the small hand stroke its feathers.

"Look at that, Sawkey. She likes children."

Sawkey tried another tack. "She'll mess your floors."

"I've raised a family." Minnie was smug. "I think I can train a goose."

He would have to give in. He knew that, so his last objection was feeble, although most important. "How'll you feed it? Geese need grain in the winter."

"I'll buy the grain, Pa," Lem promised. "I'll take some of the .22 money." For years Lem had longed and saved for a .22 rifle and always some claim would arise before he could achieve his goal.

"That's reasonable," Sawkey commented. "If you'd had a gun this afternoon and shot down this goose you'd be brag-all proud. Now you want to take your gun money to feed a bird somebody else winged."

"Lem's better off without nasty weapons." Minnie didn't favour firearms. "I'd rather see Lem caring for one of God's creatures than dealing it death. So hush up about the goose. We'll tend it and keep it. Come spring, maybe, it'll want to leave us when the flocks vee north."

"Spring's a good way off," said Sawkey, wishing it wasn't. Winter was the lean time with the Mullets.

"Golly, yes. We've got Christmas first," said Elmer, a twin.

Elroy, the other, added ". . . and the Christmas tree and the school concert."

"And Santa," piped Bermuda, the second oldest girl.

"Psssst!" came from the basket. Much as Sawkey disliked the bird, he agreed with the sentiment one hundred per cent. With a wife and eight kids the festive season brought more bills and bitterness than joy to him.

As November gave way to December his antipathy to the goose increased. Malvola Piper had had high white cheek bones and round scornful eyes; so had Lem's Malvola. Miss Piper's neck had been long; she twisted it sideways when she spoke. Malvola Goose had the same trick before uttering her psssst!

Sawkey half expected the bird to say, "Sawkey Mullet! You're the stupidest, laziest, good-for-nothing boy I ever came across. Write 'Idleness in youth brings want in old age' one hundred times."

He supposed Malvola Piper had been right, but it didn't alter his feelings towards Malvola Goose. He grumbled plenty at home, yet as he worked with the men from the Cove as they cut Christmas trees for Jethro Ward, Sawkey made loud brags about their wild pet.

"She's all but human. When the baby crawls near the stove or anywhere dangerous, Malvola heads him off like a flesh-and-blood nursemaid. She plays tricks, too. She'll untie Minnie's apron strings or sneak a handkerchief from your pocket, and then stand back and Honk! Honk! You'd swear she was laughing."

"My woman wouldn't stand for a goose dirtying up her kitchen," Jonas Carter said smugly, though his house-proud wife made his life a misery with her scrub brush and broom.

"Malvola's house broke. First off, Minnie put diapers on her. 'Twasn't needed long. She makes for the door when she wants out. Mighty smart, is Malvola."

"You don't want to sell her, do you? I've got more orders for poultry than I can fill this year." Hal Baines, who raised fowl as a sideline, put the question as a joke.

"We don't aim to kill her." But Sawkey added under his breath, "More's the pity."

Yes, Malvola was a smart goose and her intelligence brought sorrow. It happened the day the job was finished, just before Christmas.

Jethro Ward was a man of substance at the Cove. He owned the one general store, sold everything from onions and nets to cheese and cod line; he dealt in fish and lumber, insurance, boats, marine engines – anything and everything that would bring in a dollar. That year he was sending a schooner-load of Christmas trees to the States, but even the Christmas season had no effect on his selfish heart. The wages he paid the men were scandalously low. After settling the store bill, Sawkey had only sixteen dollars. Fourteen were in his wallet for Minnie; a two-dollar bill was hidden in his back pocket. A man needed spending money around Christmas.

Lem and the older children were out getting a tree and ever-greens, so the house was fairly quiet when Sawkey entered the kitchen. Minnie, the baby at her hip, was adding water to the soup and the little girls were ripping at a catalogue, watched by the feathered Malvola. The goose gave a loud Psssst! as she saw who it was. A fine welcome.

"Here's your money, Minnie." Sawkey took out his wallet. "Not much left with the store bill paid."

Minnie sighed as she counted the money. "Fourteen dollars. We'll get by, I guess. But I wish – how I wish that some year we could have a real good Christmas. One for the youngsters to remember. Store-bought presents, and chocolates, and a grand Christmas dinner."

The bill in Sawkey's pocket burned like fire and he squirmed uneasily. Still, two dollars would not buy Minnie's dream.

"Children are pampered too much, these days," he blustered. "Specially at Christmas. I declare, Minnie, you'd ruin our kids if you had a full purse."

"That'll be the day," she said tartly.

Sawkey was stung. "I do the best I can. Not my fault I've no vitality for steady work." The old excuse came quickly, but instead of Minnie's usual contrite, "I know. I'm not blaming you, Sawkey," she kept a thin-lipped silence while Malvola gave an extra loud hiss of contempt.

"Hold your tongue, you feathered witch. If I had my way we'd make dinner of your carcass. Hey! What're you up to?"

Sawkey wheeled and clapped his hand to his back pocket in consternation. Too late. Deft as a professional dip Malvola had whisked the two-dollar bill from its hiding place and was waddling across the kitchen to Minnie. She curved her long neck and gave Sawkey a wicked side glance as she laid the money in Minnie's hand.

Minnie's tone was ominous. "You kept two dollars for yourself. Shame on you, Sawkey Mullet. That you'd stoop so low!"

"I got a right to frolic money. I earned it, didn't I?"

Minnie put the bill in her apron pocket. "Not when your family needs it." She was quite put out and her eyes sparked with temper.

"Psssst!" agreed Malvola.

Sawkey turned on the goose. "You're to blame," he bellowed, snatching her up. "We've had nothing but discord and misery since you came, you eel-necked gabbler. I'll fix you!"

"Don't you kill that goose," screamed Minnie, frightening the children, who began to howl. "Don't you dare, Sawkey Mullet."

"Maybe I will, maybe I won't. I'd hate to bet she sees New Year's. Keep your two dollars." Sawkey paused at the door. "I'll get that and more from Hal Baines." He slammed the door and was gone.

Smart as Malvola was she didn't know he was taking her to her doom and, accustomed to being carried, she nestled trustingly in his arms.

It was late and dark when Sawkey returned alone – a cold night with a star-filled frosty sky and iron-bound earth. Ice had formed along the shore, muffling the tide so the ear missed the roar of shifting beach rocks, tumbling from position after each rising wave. The black shape of the house was broken by the lamp-lit kitchen window, a yellow oblong that held no welcome. Sawkey paused for a bit outside, leery of the reception he might get and knowing he deserved anything from a tongue-lash to a flung skillet.

He knew what he would do – get angry. Pound the table, scare the young ones, and act tough with Minnie. At least there would be no sneers from Malvola. He had taken care of that. Bracing himself with a gulp of frosty air, he went into the house.

"Your supper's in the warming oven," Minnie said mildly. "Must be dry as chips by now." So there wasn't going to be a ruckus, after all?

Sawkey grunted and hung up his jacket and cap with a swift look at the boys, Lem and the twins. The younger children had been put to bed so Lem and his brothers could work on the doll's house they were making for Christmas. They were so intent on their work they hardly noticed their Pa. Minnie must have talked to them.

Actually she had said, "We must make the best of it, boys. Don't hold it against your Pa. Don't sulk or be sassy – that'll only set him in his wrath. Be sorry for him. I am."

"Sorry for him? After what he's done?"

"He'll feel bad when his mad's gone."

They were used to doing what Minnie said, so they tried to obey in the next empty days. No sulks, no sass, only a sadness so thick it was like cold, heavy fog. The Mullets mourned for a Canada goose. All but Sawkey.

He tried to ignore the long faces, the way little Araby stroked a wisp of down from Malvola's basket, the break in Minnie's voice as she sang "The Vacant Chair," the way the boys steered clear of him. Nevertheless it got on his nerves.

Instead of one goose, nine humans gave him the silent reproach. The Christmas tree they had dragged from the wood leaned against the house forgotten; the paper chains lay in a box in the parlour along with the lion's paw and Canada holly wreaths that had been fun to make. The baby tangled the strings of bog cran-berries and nobody lifted a finger. All the joy of the season, and of their family life, was as dead as cold fillets.

"What ails everybody?" Sawkey stormed when he could stand it no longer. "Aren't you goin' to set up the tree? And decorate? It's more like a wake than Christmas Eve."

"It is a wake," said Lem bitterly. "Malvola's! Tomorrow at somebody's dinner table she'll have her funeral. Oh, Pa! Why did you do it? She didn't harm you." Lem's voice broke and he stum-bled towards the door so they could not see him cry.

"Wait, Lem." Sawkey put his hand on the boy's shoulder and faced his solemn, sad-eyed family.

"Malvola Piper used to tell me I was idle and worthless, that I'd be a no-account when I grew up. That there goose, looking so much like Malvola, seemed her very self, gloating about how her words had come true. It riled me – mostly 'cause it's true. I ain't much of a provider; your Ma knows that to her sorrow. I do the best I can but I've been headed the wrong way since I was a lad. I've wound up like teacher said – a do-less Sawkey Mullet, 'stead of a man of substance like Jethro Ward."

"Heaven forbid," said Minnie, piously.

"But Pa," cried Lem, "that doesn't matter. I mean, you being like you are. We wouldn't want you different. By and by me and the twins will be working and we'll have lots of money. We can have electric lights, Sunday clothes – just everything. You'll see."

Sawkey had a sudden flash of revelation. His children *would* be workers, taking a joy in toil that he had never felt, and having a hunger for possessions that he'd never known. If this were so, why should he worry over a bitter, long gone old maid, or vent his spite on a harmless bird?

He cleared his throat. "If you and the twins take a walk to the Cove and see Hal Baines, I reckon you'll find a Christmas present, Lem."

"Hal Baines?"

"Yep. She's there. I couldn't do away with her so I dickered with Hal to keep her till spring. Go and bring Malvola home for Christmas."

The Burgeo Whale

FARLEY MOWAT

Farley Mowat (b. 1921) is a prolific Canadian writer and a passionate conservationist. In 1962, he and his wife, Claire, settled in Burgeo, an isolated outport on the southeast shore of Newfoundland. In January 1967, a pregnant Fin whale weighing 80 tons became trapped in a salt-water enclosure about half a mile long, known as Aldridge's Pond. By the time Mowat had attracted the interest of the media, marine biologists, the government of Newfoundland and the general public, the whale was in danger of dying from lack of food (live herring) and infected gunshot wounds.

Unfortunately, the measures needed to save the animal seemed to infringe on the fishermen's freedom of movement. To Mowat, the entrapment of this "being of transcendental majesty and grace" came to symbolize the condition of the whole community:

> The whale was not alone in being trapped. We were all trapped with her. . . . An awesome mystery had intruded into the closely circumscribed order of our lives; one that we terrestrial bipeds could not fathom, and one, therefore, that we would react against with instinctive fear, violence, and hatred.

Because of his attempts to save the whale, Mowat generated powerful hostility. He was seen as a stranger "come here from away, telling lies about the people. Making trouble like we never had afore!"

Since 1972, when A Whale for the Killing was published, there has developed a greater appreciation for this animal. Whale watching off the British Columbia coastline is big business. Whale festivals are held to celebrate the creature through films, lectures, song and dance. The songs of the whale are recorded. Public awareness of the species' precarious position is acute. It is estimated that in the seventeenth century the Great Whales numbered 4,500,000. In 1972 their population was about 350,000. Because of environmental pollution and continued whaling by some countries, the world's whales could become extinct within the next century – "the last whale, like the last man, (will) smoke his last pipe, and then himself evaporate in the final puff."

Farley Mowat's Sea of Slaughter (1984), which he calls "my most important work," relates the sad history of man's killing of animal species along North America's coast. Claire Mowat's The Outpost People (1984) gives another view of the Burgeo community during the Mowats' five-year residence.

◄o►

Burgeo winter weather often seemed to consist of six days of storm followed by a seventh when all was forgiven, and the seventh day was almost always a Sunday. I once discussed this interesting phenomenon with the Anglican minister but he decently refused to take any credit for it.

Sunday, January 29th, was no exception. It almost seemed as if spring had come. The sun flared in a cloudless sky; there was not a breath of wind; the sea was still and the temperature soared.

Early in the morning Onie Stickland and I went off to Aldridges in his dory. We took grub and a tea kettle since I expected to spend the entire day observing the whale and noting her behaviour for the record. I hoped Onie and I would be alone with her, but there were already a number of boats moored to the rocks at the outer end of the channel when we arrived, and two or three dozen people were clustered on the ridge overlooking the Pond. I saw with relief that nobody was carrying a rifle.

We joined the watchers, among whom were several fishermen I knew, and found them seemingly content just to stand and watch the slow, steady circling of the whale. I used the opportunity to spread some propaganda about Burgeo's good luck in being host to such a beast, and how its continued well-being would help in drawing the attention of faraway government officials to a community which had been resolutely neglected for many years.

The men listened politely but they were sceptical. It was hard for them to believe that anyone outside Burgeo would be much interested in a whale. Nevertheless, there did seem to be a feeling that the whale should not be further tormented.

"They's no call for that sort of foolishness," said Harvey

Ingram, a lanky, sharp-featured fisherman, originally from Red Island. "Lave it be, says I. 'Tis doing harm to none."

Some of the others nodded in agreement and I began to wonder whether – if no help came from outside – it might be possible to rouse sufficient interest in the whale, yes, and sympathy for her, so we could take care of her ourselves.

"Poor creature has trouble enough," said one of the men who fished The Ha Ha. But then he took me down again by adding:

"Pond was full of herring first day she come in. Now we sees hardly none at all. When we first see the whale, 'twas some fat, some sleek. Now it looks poorly. Getting razor-backed, I'd say."

We were interrupted by the arrival, in a flurry of spray and whining power, of a big outboard speedboat, purchased through the catalogue by one of the young men who spent their summers on the Great Lakes freighters. He was accompanied by several of his pals, all of them sporting colourful nylon windbreakers of the sort that are almost uniforms for the habitués of small-town pool-rooms on the mainland. They came ashore, but stood apart from our soberly dressed group, talking among themselves in tones deliberately pitched high enough to reach our ears.

"We'd a had it kilt by now," said one narrow-faced youth, with a sidelong glance in my direction, "only for someone putting the Mountie onto we!"

"And that's the truth!" replied one of his companions. "Them people from away better 'tend their own business. Got no call to interfere with we." He spat in the snow to emphasize his remark.

"What we standing here for?" another asked loudly. "We's not afeared of any goddamn whale. Let's take a run onto the Pond. Might be some sport into it yet."

They ambled back to their powerboat and when the youths had clambered aboard, one of the men standing near me said quietly:

"Don't pay no heed, skipper. They's muck floats up in every place. Floats to the top and stinks, but don't mean nothin'."

It was kindly said, and I appreciated it.

By this time a steady stream of boats was converging on the Pond from Short Reach, The Harbour, and from further west. There were power dories, skiffs, longliners and even a few rowboats with youngsters at the oars. Burgeo was making the most of the fine weather to come and see its whale.

The majority of the newcomers seemed content to moor their boats with the growing armada out in the entrance cove, but several came through the channel into the Pond, following the lead of the mail-order speedboat. At first the boats which entered the Pond kept close to shore, leaving the open water to the whale. Their occupants were obviously awed by the immense bulk of the creature, and were timid about approaching anywhere near her. But by noon, by which time some thirty boats, bearing at least a hundred people, had arrived, the mood began to change.

There was now a big crowd around the south and southwest shore of the Pond. In full awareness of this audience, and fortified by lots of beer, a number of young men (and some not so young) now felt ready to show their mettle. The powerful boat which had been the first to enter suddenly accelerated to full speed and roared directly across the Pond only a few yards behind the whale as she submerged. Some of the people standing along the shore raised a kind of ragged cheer, and within minutes the atmosphere had completely – and frighteningly – altered.

More and more boats started up their engines and nosed into the Pond. Five or six of the fastest left the security of the shores and darted out into the middle. The reverberation of many engines began to merge into a sustained roar, a baleful and ferocious sound, intensified by the echoes from the surrounding cliffs. The leading powerboat became more daring and snarled across the whale's wake at close to twenty knots, dragging a high rooster-tail of spray.

The whale was now no longer moving leisurely in great circles, coming up to breathe at intervals of five or ten minutes. She had begun to swim much faster and more erratically as she attempted to avoid the several boats which were chivvying her. The swirls of water from her flukes became much more agitated as she veered sharply from side to side. She was no longer able to clear her lungs with the usual two or three blows after every dive, but barely had time to suck in a single breath before being driven down again. Her hurried surfacings consequently became more and more frequent even as the sportsmen, gathering courage because the whale showed no sign of retaliation, grew braver and braver. Two of the fastest boats began to circle her at full throttle, like a pair of malevolent water beetles.

Meanwhile, something rather terrible was taking place in the emotions of many of the watchers ringing the Pond. The mood of passive curiosity had dissipated, to be replaced by one of hungry anticipation. Looking into the faces around me, I recognized the same avid air of expectation which contorts the faces of a prizefight audience into primal masks.

At this juncture the blue hull of the R.C.M.P. launch appeared in the entrance cove. Onie and I jumped aboard the dory and intercepted her. I pleaded with Constable Murdoch for help.

"Some of these people have gone wild! They're going to drive the whale ashore if they don't drown her first. You have to put a stop to it . . . order them out of the Pond!"

The constable shook his head apologetically.

"Sorry. I can't do that. They aren't breaking any law, you know. I can't do anything unless the local authorities ask me to. But we'll take the launch inside and anchor in the middle of the Pond. Maybe that'll discourage them a bit."

He was a nice young man but out of his element and determined not to do anything which wasn't "in the book." He was well within his rights; and I certainly overstepped mine when, in my distress, I intimated that he was acting like a coward. He made no reply, but quietly told Danny to take the police boat in.

Onie and I followed them through the channel, then we turned along the southwest shore where I hailed several men in boats, pleading with them to leave the whale alone. Some made no response. One of them, a middle-aged merchant, gave me a derisive grin and deliberately accelerated his engine to drown out my voice. Even the elder fishermen standing on shore now seemed more embarrassed by my attitude than sympathetic. I was slow to realize it but the people gathered at Aldridges Pond had sensed that a moment of high drama was approaching and, if it was to be a tragic drama, so much the better.

Having discovered that there was nothing to fear either from the whale or from the police, the speedboat sportsmen began to make concerted efforts to herd the great beast into the shallow easterly portion of the Pond. Three boats succeeded in cornering her in a small bight, and when she turned violently to avoid them, she grounded for half her length on a shelf of rock.

There followed a stupendous flurry of white water as her immense flukes lifted clear and beat upon the surface. She reared forward, raising her whole head into view, then turned on her side so that one huge flipper pointed skyward. I had my binoculars on her and for a moment could see all of her lower belly, and the certain proof that she was female. Then slowly and, it seemed, painfully, she rolled clear of the rock.

As she slid free, there was a hubbub from the crowd on shore, a sound amounting almost to a roar, that was audible even over the snarl of engines. It held a note of insensate fury that seemed to inflame the boatmen to even more vicious attacks upon the now panic-stricken whale.

Making no attempt to submerge, she fled straight across the Pond in the direction of the eastern shallows where there were, at that moment, no boats or people. The speedboats raced close beside her, preventing her from changing course. She seemed to make a supreme effort to outrun them and then, with horrifying suddenness, she hit the muddy shoals and drove over them until she was aground for her whole length.

The Pond erupted in pandemonium. Running and yelling people leapt into boats of all shapes and sizes and these began converging on the stranded animal. I recognized the doctor team – the deputy mayor of Burgeo and his councillor wife – aboard one small longliner. I told Onie to lay the dory alongside them and I scrambled over the longliner's rail while she was still under way. By this time I was so enraged as to be almost inarticulate. Furiously I *ordered* the deputy mayor to tell the constable to clear the Pond.

He was a man with a very small endowment of personal dignity. I had outraged what dignity he did possess. He pursed his soft, red lips and replied:

"What would be the use of that? The whale is going to die anyway. Why should I interfere?" He turned his back and busied himself recording the whale's "last moments" with his expensive movie camera.

The exchange had been overheard, for the boats were now packed tightly into the cul-de-sac and people were scrambling from boat to boat, or along the shore itself, to gain a better view. There was a murmur of approval for the doctor and then someone yelled, gloatingly:

"Dat whale is finished, byes! It be ashore for certain now! Good riddance is what I says!"

Indeed, the whale's case looked hopeless. She was aground in less than twelve feet of water; and the whole incredible length of her, from the small of the tail almost to her nose, was exposed to view. The tide was on the ebb and if she remained where she was for even as little as half an hour, she would be doomed to die where she lay. Yet she was not struggling. Now that no boats were tormenting her, she seemed to ignore the human beings who fringed the shore not twenty feet away. I had the sickening conviction that she had given up; that the struggle for survival had become too much.

My anguish was so profound that when I saw three men step out into the shallows and begin heaving rocks at her half-submerged head, I went berserk. Scrambling to the top of the longliner's deckhouse, I screamed imprecations at them. Faces turned toward

me and, having temporarily focused attention on myself, I launched into a wild tirade.

This was a *female* whale, I cried. She might be and probably was pregnant. This attack on her was a monstrous, despicable act of cruelty. If, I threatened, everyone did not instantly get to hell out of Aldridges Pond and leave the whale be, I would make it my business to blacken Burgeo's name from one end of Canada to the other.

Calming down a little, I went on to promise that if the whale survived she would make Burgeo famous. "You'll get your damned highway!" I remember yelling. "Television and all the rest of it . . ." God knows what else I might have said or promised if the whale had not herself intervened.

Somebody shouted in surprise; and we all looked. She was moving.

She was turning – infinitely slowly – sculling with her flippers and gently agitating her flukes. We Lilliputians watched silent and incredulous as the vast Gulliver inched around until she was facing out into the Pond. Then slowly, slowly, almost imperceptibly, she drifted off the shoals and slid from sight beneath the glittering surface.

I now realize that she had not been in danger of stranding herself permanently. On the contrary, she had taken the one course open to her and had deliberately sought out the shallows where she could quite literally catch her breath, free from the harassment of the motorboats. But, at the time, her escape from what appeared to be mortal danger almost seemed to savour of the miraculous. Also, as if by another miracle, it radically altered the attitude of the crowd, suddenly subduing the mood of feverish excitement. People began to climb quietly back into their boats. One by one the boats moved off toward the south channel, and within twenty minutes Aldridges Pond was empty of all human beings except Onie and me.

It was an extraordinary exodus. Nobody seemed to be speaking to anybody else . . . and not one word was said to me. Some people averted their eyes as they passed our dory. I do not think this was because of any guilt they may have felt – and many of them *did* feel guilty – it was because *I* had shamed *them*, as a group, as a community, as a people . . . and had done so publicly. The stranger in their midst had spoken his heart and displayed his rage and scorn. We could no longer pretend we understood each other. We had become strangers, one to the other.

My journal notes, written late that night, reflect my bewilderment and my sense of loss.

". . . they are essentially good people. I know that, but what sickens me is their simple failure to resist the impulse of savagery . . . they seem to be just as capable of being utterly loathsome as the bastards from the cities with their high-powered rifles and telescopic sights and their mindless compulsion to slaughter everything alive, from squirrels to elephants . . . I admired them so much because I saw them as a natural people, living in at least some degree of harmony with the natural world. Now they seem nauseatingly anxious to renounce all that and throw themselves into the stinking quagmire of our society which has perverted everything natural within itself, and is now busy destroying everything natural outside itself. How can they be so bloody stupid? How could *I* have been so bloody stupid?"

Bitter words . . . bitter, and unfair; but I had lost my capacity for objectivity and was ruled, now, by irrational emotions. I was no longer willing, or perhaps not able, to understand the people of Burgeo; to comprehend them as they really were, as men and women who were also victims of forces and circumstances of whose effects they remained unconscious. I had withdrawn my compassion from them, in hurt and ignorance. Now I bestowed it all upon the whale.

The Cat That Went
to Trinity

◄○►

ROBERTSON DAVIES

Robertson Davies (1913-1995), born in Thamesville, Ontario, and educated at Upper Canada College, Queen's University, Kingston, and Balliol College, Oxford, was internationally known as a novelist, dramatist, essayist and critic. During his long, full life he was an actor with England's Old Vic Company, editor of Saturday Night *magazine, editor then publisher of the Peterborough* Examiner, *an active supporter of the Stratford (Ontario) Shakespeare Festival, a university professor and the first Master of Massey College, University of Toronto. A commentator suggested that his High Church Toryism, tweed suits, flowing beard (of Santa Claus proportions) and witty conversation well qualified him for the latter position.*

The title of a scrapbook made fifty years ago – "Clippings Relating to Oddities, Absurdities, Curiosa, Crime and Suicide, and Strange Manifestations of the Holy Spirit" – foreshadows a long-time interest in the esoteric and off-beat, an interest that makes many of his short stories and novels stimulatingly bizarre. Among his more than thirty books are three trilogies – the Salterton, the Deptford and the Cornish. The latter group of novels, consisting of The Rebel Angels *(1981),* What's Bred in the Bone *(1985) and* The Lyre of Orpheus *(1988), are centred on a fictional University of Toronto College, the College of Saint John and the Holy Ghost, known as "Spook." They reveal the same idiosyncratic, competitive and obsessive academic life that is found in "The Cat That Went to Trinity." This story is one of a series of supernatural tales that Davies traditionally created for Massey College's Gaudy Night celebration. It combines in a characteristic way satire, horror, parody and the macabre. Davies lamented the fact that our science-dominated, materialistic age is unsympathetic to a belief in ghosts. "Surely," he asked, "it is a little conceited of us to suppose that we are the only spiritual inhabitants of this world." At his funeral service in the Chapel of Trinity College, the Trinity cat was mentioned.*

◄○►

E very Autumn when I meet my new classes, I look them over to see if there are any pretty girls in them. This is not a custom peculiar to me: all professors do it. A pretty girl is something on which I can rest my eyes with pleasure while another student is reading a carefully researched but uninspiring paper.

This year, in my seminar on the Gothic Novel, there was an exceptionally pretty girl, whose name was Elizabeth Lavenza. I thought it a coincidence that this should also be the name of the heroine of one of the novels we were about to study – no less a work than Mary Shelley's celebrated romance *Frankenstein*. When I mentioned it to her she brushed it aside as of no significance.

"I was born in Geneva," said she, "where lots of people are called Lavenza."

Nevertheless, it lingered in my mind, and I mentioned it to one of my colleagues, who is a celebrated literary critic.

"You have coincidence on the brain," he said. "Ever since you wrote that book – *Fourth Dimension* or whatever it was called – you've talked about nothing else. Forget it."

I tried, but I couldn't forget it. It troubled me even more after I had met the new group of Junior Fellows in this College, for one of them was young Einstein, who was studying Medical Biophysics. He was a brilliant young man, who came to us with glowing recommendations; some mention was made of a great-uncle of his, an Albert Einstein, whose name meant nothing to me, though it appeared to have special significance in the scientific world. It was young Mr. Einstein's given names that roused an echo in my consciousness, for he was called Victor Frank.

For those among you who have not been reading Gothic Novels lately, I may explain that in Mrs. Shelley's book *Frankenstein, or The Modern Prometheus*, the hero's name is also Victor, and the girl he loved was Elizabeth Lavenza. The richness of coincidence might trouble a mind less disposed to such reflection than mine. I held my peace, for I had been cowed by what my friend the literary critic had said. But I was dogged by apprehension, for I know the disposition of the atmosphere of Massey College to constellate extraordinary elements. Thus, cowed and dogged, I kept my eyes open for what might happen.

It was no more than a matter of days when Fate added another figure to this coincidental pattern, and Fate's instrument was none other than my wife. It is our custom to entertain the men of the College to dinner, in small groups, and my wife invites a few girls to each of these occasions to lighten what might otherwise be a too exclusively academic atmosphere. The night that Frank Einstein appeared in our drawing-room he maintained his usual reserved – not to say morose – demeanour until Elizabeth Lavenza entered the room. Their meeting was in one sense, a melodramatic cliché. But we must remember that things become clichés because they are of frequent occurrence, and powerful impact. Everything fell out as a thoroughly bad writer might describe it. Their eyes met across the room. His glance was electric; hers ecstatic. The rest of the company seemed to part before them as he moved to her side. He never left it all evening. She had eyes for no other. From time to time his eyes rose in ardour, while hers fell in modest transport. This rising and falling of eyes was so portentously and swooningly apparent that one or two of our senior guests felt positively unwell, as though aboard ship. My heart sank. My wife's, on the contrary, was up-lifted. As I passed her during the serving of the meal I hissed, "This is Fate." "There is no armour against Fate," she hissed in return. It is a combination of words not easily hissed, but she hissed it.

We had an unusually fine Autumn, as you will recall, and there was hardly a day that I did not see Frank and Elizabeth sitting on one of the benches in the quad, sometimes talking, but usually looking deep into each other's eyes, their foreheads touching. They did it so much that they both became slightly cross-eyed, and my dismay mounted. I determined if humanly possible to avert some disastrous outcome (for I assure you that my intuition and my knowledge of the curious atmosphere of this College both oppressed me with boding) and I did all that lay in my power. I heaped work on Elizabeth Lavenza; I demanded the ultimate from her in reading of the Gothic Novel, as a means both of keeping her from Frank, and of straightening her vision.

Alas, how puny are our best efforts to avert a foreordained event! One day I saw Frank in the quad, sitting on the bench alone, reading a book. Pretending nonchalance, I sat beside him. "And what are you reading, Mr. Einstein?" I said in honeyed tones.

Taciturn as always, he held out the book for me to see. It was *Frankenstein*. "Liz said I ought to read it," he said.

"And what do you make of it?" said I, for I am always interested in the puny efforts of art to penetrate the thoroughly scientific mind. His answer astonished me.

"Not bad at all," said he. "The Medical Biophysics aspect of the plot is very old-fashioned, of course. I mean when the hero makes that synthetic human being out of scraps from slaughter-houses. We could do better than that now. A lot better," he added, and I thought he seemed to be brooding on nameless possibilities. I decided to change the line of our conversation. I began to talk about the College, and some of the successes and failures we had met with in the past.

Among the failures I mentioned our inability to keep a College Cat. In the ten years of our existence we have had several cats here, but not one of them has remained with us. They all run away, and there is strong evidence that they all go to Trinity. I thought at one time that they must be Anglican cats, and they objected to our œcumenical chapel. I went to the length of getting a Persian cat, raised in the Zoroastrian faith, but it only lasted two days. There is a fine Persian rug in Trinity Chapel. Our most recent cat had been christened Episcopuss, in the hope that this thoroughly Anglican title would content it; furthermore, the Lionel Massey fund provided money to treat the cat to a surgical operation which is generally thought to lift a cat's mind above purely sectarian considerations. But it, too, left us for Trinity. Rationalists in the College suggested that Trinity has more, and richer, garbage than we have, but I still believe our cats acted on religious impulse.

As I spoke of these things Frank Einstein became more animated than I had ever known him. "I get it," he said; "you want a cat that has been specifically programmed for Massey. An œcumenical cat, highly intelligent so that it prefers graduates to undergraduates, and incapable of making messes in the Round Room. With a few hours of computer time it oughtn't to be too difficult."

I looked into his eyes – though from a greater distance than was usual to Elizabeth Lavenza – and what I saw there caused a familiar shudder to convulse my entire being. It is the shudder I feel when I know, for a certainty, that Massey College is about to be the scene of yet another macabre event.

Nevertheless, in the pressure of examinations and lectures, I forgot my uneasiness, and might perhaps have dismissed the matter from my mind if two further interrelated circumstances – I dare not use the word coincidence in this case – had not aroused my fears again. One autumn morning, reading *The Globe and*

Mail, my eye was caught by an item, almost lost at the bottom of a column, which bore the heading "Outrage at Pound"; it appeared that two masked bandits, a man and a woman, had held up the keeper of the pound at gun-point, while seizing no less than twelve stray cats. Later that same day I saw Frank and Elizabeth coming through the College gate, carrying a large and heavy sack. From the sack dripped a substance which I recognized, with horror, as blood. I picked up a little of it on the tip of my finger; a hasty corpuscle count confirmed my suspicion that the blood was not human.

Night after night in the weeks that followed, I crept down to my study to look across the quad and see if a light was burning in Frank Einstein's room. Invariably it was so. And one morning, when I had wakened early and was standing on my balcony, apostrophizing the dawn, Elizabeth Lavenza stole past me from the College's main gate, her face marked, not by those lineaments of slaked desire so common among our visitors at such an hour, but by the pallor and fatigue of one well-nigh exhausted by intellectual work of the most demanding sort.

The following night I awoke from sleep at around two o'clock with a terrifying apprehension that something was happening in the College which I should investigate. Shouts, the sound of loud music, the riot of late revellers – these things do not particularly disturb me, but there is a quality of deep silence which I know to be the accompaniment of evil. Wearily and reluctantly I rose, wrapped myself in a heavy dressing-gown, and made my way into the quadrangle and there – yes, it was as I had feared – the eerie gleam from Frank Einstein's room was the only light to guide me. For there was a thick fog hanging over the University, and even the

240 / ROBERTSON DAVIES

cruel light through the arrow-slits of the Robarts Library and the faery radiance from OISE were hidden.

Up to his room I climbed, and tapped on the door. It had not been locked, and my light knock caused it to swing open and there – never can I forget my shock and revulsion at what I saw! – there were Frank and Elizabeth crouched over a table upon which lay an ensanguined form. I burst upon them.

"What bloody feast is this?" I shouted. "Monsters, fiends, cannibals, what do I behold?"

"Shhh," said Elizabeth; "Frank's busy."

"I'm making your cat," said Frank.

"Cat," I shrieked, almost beside myself; "that is no cat. It's as big as a donkey. What cat are you talking about?"

"The Massey College cat," said Frank. "And it is going to be the greatest cat you have ever seen."

I shall not trouble you with a detailed report of the conversation that followed. What emerged was this: Frank, beneath the uncommunicative exterior of a scientist, had a kindly heart, and he had been touched by the unlucky history of Massey College and its cats. "What you said was," said he to me, "that the College never seemed to get the right cat. To you, with your simple, emotional, literary approach to the problem, this was an insuperable difficulty: to my finely organized biophysical sensibility, it was simply a matter of discovering what kind of cat was wanted, and producing it. Not by the outmoded method of selective breeding, but by the direct creation of the Ideal College Cat, or ICC as I came to think of it. Do you remember that when you talked to me about it I was reading the crazy book Liz was studying with you, about the fellow who made a man? Do you remember what he said?

'Whence did the principle of life proceed? It was a bold question, and one which has ever been considered as a mystery; yet with how many things are we upon the brink of becoming acquainted, if cowardice or carelessness did not restrain our enquiries.' That was written in 1818. Since then the principle of life has become quite well known, but most scientists are afraid to work on the knowledge they have. You remember that the fellow in the book decided to make a man, but he found the work too fiddly if he made a man of ordinary size, so he decided to make a giant. Me too. A cat of ordinary size is a nuisance, so I decided to multiply the dimensions by twelve. And like the fellow in the book I got my materials and went to work. Here is your cat, about three-quarters finished."

The fatal weakness, the tragic flaw, in my character is foolish good-nature, and that, combined with an uninformed but lively scientific curiosity, led me into what was, I now perceive, a terrible mistake. I was so interested in what Frank was doing that I allowed him to go ahead, and instead of sleeping at nights I crept up to his room, where Frank and Elizabeth allowed me, after I had given my promise not to interfere or touch anything, to sit in a corner and watch them. Those weeks were perhaps the most intensely lived that I have ever known. Beneath my eyes the ICC grew and took form. By day the carcass was kept in the freezer at Rochdale, where Elizabeth had a room; each night Frank warmed it up and set to work.

The ICC had many novel features which distinguished it from the ordinary domestic cat. Not only was it as big as twelve ordinary cats; it had twelve times the musculature. Frank said proudly that when it was finished it would be able to jump right over the

College buildings. Another of its beauties was that it possessed a novel means of elimination. The trouble with all cats is that they seem to be housebroken, but in moments of stress or laziness they relapse into an intolerable bohemianism which creates problems for the cleaning staff. In a twelve-power cat this could be a serious defect. But Frank's cat was made with a small shovel on the end of its tail with which it could, once a week, remove its own ashes and deposit them behind the College in the parking-space occupied by *The Varsity*, where, it was assumed, they would never be noticed. I must hasten to add that the cat was made to sustain itself on a diet of waste-paper, of which we have plenty, and that what it produced in the manner I have described was not unlike confetti.

But the special beauty of the ICC was that it could talk. This, in the minds of Frank and Elizabeth, was its great feature as a College pet. Instead of mewing monotonously when stroked, it would be able to enter into conversation with the College men, and as we pride ourselves on being a community of scholars, it was to be provided with a class of conversation and a vocabulary, infinitely superior to that of, for instance, a parrot.

This was Elizabeth's special care, and because she was by this time deep in my course on the Gothic Novel she decided, as a compliment to me, to so program the cat that it would speak in the language appropriate to that *genre* of literature. I was not so confident about this refinement as were Frank and Elizabeth, for I knew more about Gothic Novels than they, and have sometimes admitted to myself that they can be wordy. But as I have told you, I was a party to this great adventure only in the character of a spectator, and I was not to interfere. So I held my peace, hoping that the cat would, in the fulness of time, do the same.

At last the great night came, when the cat was to be invested with life. I sat in my corner, my eyes fixed upon the form which Frank was gradually melting out with Elizabeth's electric hair-dryer. It was a sight to strike awe into the boldest heart.

I never dared to make my doubts about the great experiment known to Frank and Elizabeth, but I may tell you that my misgivings were many and acute. I am a creature of my time in that I fully understand that persons of merely aesthetic bias and training, like myself, should be silent in the presence of men of science, who know best about everything. But it was plain to me that the ICC was hideous. Not only was it the size of twelve cats, but the skins of twelve cats had been made to serve as its outer envelope. Four of these cats had been black, four were white, and four were of a marmalade colour. Frank, who liked things to be orderly, had arranged them so that the cat was piebald in mathematically exact squares. Because no ordinary cat's eyes would fit into the huge skull the eyes of a goat had been obtained – I dared not ask how – and as everyone knows, a goat's eyes are flat and have an uncanny oblong pupil. The teeth had been secured at a bargain rate from a denturist, and as I looked at them I knew why dentists say that these people must be kept in check. The tail, with the shovel at the end of it, was disagreeably naked. Its whiskers were like knitting needles. Indeed, the whole appearance of the cat was monstrous and diabolical. In the most exact sense of the words, it was the damnedest thing you ever saw. But Frank had a mind above appearances and to Elizabeth, so beautiful herself, whatever Frank did was right.

The moment had arrived when this marvel of science was to be set going. I know that Frank was entirely scientific, but to my old-fashioned eye he looked like an alchemist as, with his dressing-gown floating around him, he began to read formulae out of a notebook, and Elizabeth worked switches and levers at his command. Suddenly there was a flash, of lightning it seemed to me, and I knew that we had launched the ICC upon its great adventure.

"Come here and look," said Frank. I crept forward, half-afraid yet half-elated that I should be witness to such a triumph of medical biophysics. I leaned over the frightful creature, restraining my revulsion. Slowly, dreamily, the goat's eyes opened and focussed upon me.

"My Creator!" screamed the cat in a very loud voice, that agreed perfectly with the hideousness of its outward person. "A thousand, thousand blessings be upon Thee. Hallowed be Thy name! Thy kingdom come! O rapture, rapture thus to behold the golden dawn!" With which words the cat leapt upon an electric lamp and ate the bulb.

To say that I recoiled is to trifle with words. I leapt backward into a chair and cringed against the wall. The cat pursued me, shrieking Gothic praise and endearment. It put out its monstrous tongue and licked my hand. Imagine, if you can, the tongue of a cat which is twelve cats rolled into one. It was weeks before the skin-graft made necessary by this single caress was completed. But I am ahead of my story.

"No, no," I cried; "my dear animal, listen to reason. I am not your Creator. Not in the least. You owe the precious gift of life to my young friend here."

I waved my bleeding hand toward Frank. In their rapture he and Elizabeth were locked in a close embrace. That did it. Horrid, fiendish jealousy swept through the cat's whole being. All its twelve coats stood on end, the goat's eyes glared with fury, and its shovel tail lashed like that of a tiger. It sprang at Elizabeth, and with a single stroke of its powerful forepaws flung her to the ground.

I am proud to think that in that terrible moment I remembered what to do. I have always loved circuses, and I know that no trainer of tigers ever approaches his beasts without a chair in his hand. I seized up a chair and, in the approved manner, drove the monstrous creature into a corner. But what I said was not in tune with my action, or the high drama of the moment. I admit it frankly; my words were inadequate.

"You mustn't harm Miss Lavenza," I said, primly; "she is Mr. Einstein's fiancée."

But Frank's words – or rather his single word – were even more inadequate than my own. "Scat!" he shouted, kneeling by the bleeding form of his fainting beloved.

Elizabeth was to blame for programming that cat with a vocabulary culled from the Gothic Novel. "Oh, Frankenstein," it yowled, in that tremendous voice; "be not equitable to every other and trample upon me alone, to whom thy justice and even thy clemency and affection is most due. Remember that I am thy creature; I ought to be thy Adam; dub me not rather the fallen angel, whom thou drivest hence only because I love – nay reverence – thee. Jealousy of thy love makes me a fiend. Make me happy, and I shall once more be virtuous."

There is something about that kind of talk that influences everybody that hears it. I was astonished to hear Frank – who was generally contented with the utilitarian vocabulary of the scientific man – say: "Begone! I will not hear you. There can be no community between thee and me; we are enemies. Cursed be the day, abhorred devil, in which you first saw the light! You have left me no power to consider whether I am just to you or not. Begone! Relieve me of the sight of your detested form!"

Elizabeth was not the most gifted of my students, and the cat's next words lacked something of the true Gothic rhetoric. "You mean you don't love your own dear little Pussikins best," it whined. But Frank was true to the Gothic vein. "This lady is the mistress of my affections, and I acknowledge no Pussikins before her," he cried.

The cat was suddenly a picture of desolation, of rejection, of love denied. Its vocabulary moved back into high gear. "Thus I relieve thee, my creator. Thus I take from thee a sight which you abhor. Farewell!" And with one gigantic bound it leapt through the window into the quadrangle, and I heard the thunderous sound as the College gate was torn from its hinges.

I know where it went, and I felt deeply sorry for Trinity.

Acknowledgements

Every effort was made to trace owners of copyright material reprinted in this collection. Information with respect to copyright material should be sent to the publisher.

"Luck of Life." From *Umingmuk of the Barrens* by Francis Dickie. © Copyright 1927 by Francis Dickie. Reprinted by permission of Hodder Headline plc.

"A Motherless Cub." From *Derry of Totem Creek* by Hubert Evans. Reprinted by permission of Elizabeth Bakewell and Joan Winter.

"The Dark-eyed Doe." From *Willowdale* by Kerry Wood (Toronto: McClelland & Stewart, 1956). © Copyright 1956 by Kerry Wood. Reprinted by permission.

"Winter Dog." From *As Birds Bring Forth the Sun* by Alistair MacLeod. Used by permission of McClelland & Stewart Inc., Toronto, *The Canadian Publishers.*

"A Boy and His Dog." From *Paradise Cafe and Other Stories* by Martha Brooks. (Saskatoon: Thistledown Press, 1988). Reprinted by permission of Thistledown Press.

"The Black Stallion and the Red Mare." By Gladys Francis Lewis. Reprinted by permission.

"Jeannot the Crow." Excerpt from *Enchanted Summer* by Gabrielle Roy. © 1972 by Gabrielle Roy. Translated from the French by Joyce Marshall. Reprinted with permission of Fonds Gabrielle Roy.

"The Burgeo Whale." Excerpt from *A Whale for the Killing* by Farley Mowat (Toronto: McClelland & Stewart, 1972). © Copyright 1972 by Farley Mowat. Reprinted by permission.

"The Cat That Went to Trintiy." From *One Half of Robertson Davies* by Robertson Davies (Toronto: Macmillan, 1977). Reprinted by permission.